The Deprived, The Disabled, and The Fullness of Life

The Deprived, The Disabled, and The Fullness of Life

By
_____

Austin Smith
Virginia Harrison
Stanley Hauerwas
Harold Wilke
Henry B. Betts

Edited by
_____

Flavian Dougherty

Michael Glazier, Inc.

Wilmington, Delaware

First published in 1984 by Michael Glazier, Inc., 1723 Delaware Avenue, Wilmington, Delaware 19806

Library of Congress Card Catalog Number: 84-81242
International Standard Book Numbers:
   THE DEPRIVED 0-089453-442-4

Cover design by Robert McGovern
Typogrphy by Richard Rein Smith
Printed in the United States of America

CONTENTS

THE CONTRIBUTORS

AUSTIN SMITH, C.P., PhD, is the Director of an Inner City Mission and a Prison Chaplain in Liverpool England, the city of his birth. Formerly a professor of philosophy, he has lectured extensively throughout England, Europe and the U.S. on the human and civil rights of the poor, minorities, prisoners and the voiceless. He has published extensively in periodicals, and recently authored the book: *Passion For The Inner-City*. He also serves as a member of Britain's National Commission for Racial Equality.

VIRGINIA HARRISON, PhD, Cand. is Associate Professor of Biology at Webster College, St. Louis, Mo. Among the courses she teaches are Medical Genetics, Neurobiology, Developmental Biology, Advanced Physiology and Biomedical Ethics. Virginia was born with spina bifida, and as a result, has had to use a wheelchair and crutches throughout her life. In 1963, she helped found a worldwide spiritual movement run by and for persons with handicaps, known as Victim Missionaries.

STANLEY M. HAUERWAS, PhD, is a professor of Ethics and Theology at the University of Notre Dame. He is a graduate of Yale Divinity and Graduate School. He has published on such issues as situation ethics, abortion, euthanasia, the care of mentally handicapped persons and political ethics in several books, as well as articles in leading journals of theology, ethics and politics. He has been a legal guardian of persons who are mentally disabled.

HAROLD WILKE, PhD, is an armless ordained minister in the United Church of Christ. His career includes service as Pastor, minister of a university church, Armed Forces chaplain, Director of the Council for the Ministry in the United Church, Adjunct Professor at Union Theological Seminary, faculty member of the Menninger Foundation School of Psychiatry, author and internationally known lecturer, organizer and consultant. Dr. Wilke founded an ecumenical organization, "The Healing Community" to assist various alienated groups into the mainstream of church and society.

HENRY B. BETTS, MD, is internationally known for his work in rehabilitative medicine. He is Chairman, Professor and attending medical staff physician at Northwestern Memorial Hospital, Dept. of Rehabilitative Medicine and Medical Director at the Rehabilitation Institute, Chicago. Dr. Betts serves on numerous Boards of Directors, e.g., Chicago Bar Association, The

National Office on Disability, Washington, D.C., The National Committee on Arts for the Handicapped. He is the recipient of many honors and is constantly sought for lectures, TV appearances and radio presentations.

FLAVIAN DOUGHERTY, a member of the Passionist Community at Catholic Theological Union in Chicago, is the U.S. Director of Stauros International, an organization which conducts studies and projects on various aspects of human suffering. He has conducted three International Congresses on The Meaning of Human Suffering, a symposium at the United Nations in N.Y. in preparation for the International Year of Disabled Persons, and is on the Board of Directors of Advocates for the Handicapped in Chicago.

INTRODUCTION

Pain, Suffering and "Marginal Life" was the theme of an International Congress in June 1983. As the Director of that Congress, I was, and am, constantly asked two questions: "what do you mean by "marginal life"?", and, "what is the connection with pain and suffering?" I usually answer the second question first by observing that it is the phenomenon of pain and suffering that brings to consciousness the critical issues in the lives of individuals and in society at large. It is pain and suffering underlying the current questions of who should live and who should die. It is pain and suffering which prompt all major social changes, as in the case of slavery and all civil rights struggles. It is pain and suffering which are used as yardsticks to judge the quality of life. It is pain and suffering which challenges the authenticity of every ethical and religious system.

My second answer is that "marginal life" is an expression frequently applied to various groups of people who do not fit into classifications such as "normal" or "mainstream". Most prominent among these are the chronically poor, living on the "margins" of society, and disabled persons, physically and mentally, whose lives are described as having only a "marginal" existence.

The opportunity to address the topic, both for the Congress participants and for publication, was eagerly seized by five remarkably gifted persons, two of whom have been personally stigmatized as having a "marginal" existence, and three who have been working for many years with those consigned to the "margins" of society. From their personal experiences, and their professional specialties, they have given us profound and valuable insights in these pages.

As one reads their words, it becomes strikingly obvious that they understand the term "marginal", as applied to persons, subtly pernicious. This is so because they see life, at every stage, as precious in itself, with no intrinsic marginality to it. Furthermore, and this is of supreme importance, they see that the term obscures the fact that it is others, whether in individual acts or social systems, who create and maintain the margins.

Finally, they do us the service of raising our consciousness on how we can address, and perhaps overcome, the pain and suffering of those who have been "marginalized".

Flavian Dougherty, C.P.
Editor

MARGINALISM AND INSTITUTIONALISM

by

Austin Smith

Nostalgia for the unity and harmony which existed in a nation in days of war is often expressed in the critical and troubled days of peace. It is the articulation of a highly seductive philosophy of life. This came home to me, not without some force, during the Falklands conflict. The period of this conflict, not to mention the period since, was a dangerous psychological time for contemporary British history. Those of us who had been brought up in the midst of World War II could catch the mood of the nation very quickly. One had an eerie feeling of being thrown back over forty years in time. Objective debate about the whole issue began to recede into the background. Contrary opinions took to whispering.

The silence of debate, the fear one had of expressing a contrary opinion, bordered on the sinister. One felt "propagandized" into silence. There was a superficial sense of a nation, torn to tatters with economic problems and frayed at the edges with political factions, finding identity in unity and harmony around a common cause. But what surfaced, above all things, was a certain predictable "privatization".

As the conflict progressed, individual commitment to and immersion in a common cause were invoked as the examples for a road forward and a means to total solutions for our social, political and economic ills. "We are great again! We are great because individuals have rallied to the common aim." This is a dangerous and highly distracting philosophy of life. Wars are essentially institutional games. They may be graced with the language and the symbol of the personal, but in essence they are institutional. Even should war be initiated by one person in the name of personal ambition, it is carried through to its relentless conclusion in an institutionalized manner. To dress up the end of war by crimes of the individuals who began and carried through the conflict, or to present to the public conscience examples of great personal fortitude may well be commendable, but such approaches should not distract us from war's institutional nature.

Wars are not started, conducted or finalized by individual endeavor. In war individuals have submitted their lives to the political, and more specifically, military institutions. They have done so because such submission is seen at best as presenting an ideal to fight for, or, at worst, as the only means of survival. The latter is important because it is in the institution that the expertise rests for the personal and communal safe conduct of the war. In a word, to privatize war is to conduct a frightening and great deception. It is not pursued by individuals even though far too many individuals end up as its victims.

I begin in this way to highlight the dangers of a "privatization philosophy" of life. I begin with the example of war, the greatest reality of our times, to shock us out of a "privatization philosophy".

The Self and the Other

There is a sense in which I stand alone before God and humanity. There is a sense in which I must surrender myself as a individual to God and humanity. Individuals commit murder and rape and individuals compose poetry and music. My fellow human beings look to me as a solitary human being to declare my personal intent face to face with the major questions of life. In fact one of life's deeper tragedies is that too few do declare their intent about life's great questions and issues.

In the Christian ethic there is a profound precedent for this. I refer obviously to the demand of God that Jesus personally go through the darkness of death for the sake of the Kingdom's values. God, in the Judaic-Christian tradition, has been shown as a jealous God demanding personal capitulation. Yet, on the one hand, individuals only find enrichment in so far as they exist with the other and, on the other hand, individuals are daily circumscribed and socially controlled by the institutions and structures which a society has developed historically. Privatization and the tendency to over-privatize are highly dangerous. They are dangerous for a number of reasons. I mention but three.

One has to do with the tendency in individuals to escape from the ambiguities of human existence by setting up personal talismans, they could be called idols, as the answers to all life's intricate and intimate problems. Something or someone is seen as the panacea for all ills and doubts. Everything, emotionally and intellectually, is invested in that panacea.

Another reason, and one with which we are well acquainted historically, is that which sets up the individual as an absolute. In such a format of thinking the world's agonies can be worked out by myself or, in Christian terms, by myself and God in private commune. Privatization in this example uses personal insight or personal belief in God as the answer to the unravelling of the tangled web of human choices and decisions.

But lastly is the reason, and perhaps the most dangerous, which fails to see that I am by nature part of the "other". I have, in social, political and economic terms, been consciously or unconsciously drawn into a web of behavior patterns and symbols historically initiated, developed and refined. In a word, I am "thrown" into the life of the "other" and I am institutionalized.

I cannot understand, still less cure, the pain and suffering of marginalization if I do not grasp this final reason in the danger of privatization. The pain and suffering of the marginalized, and let it be clear that marginalization is in itself pain and suffering, has its roots not only in the uncaring of individuals but in the social, political and economic institutions of our world. Our institutions have controlled too many in their social thinking. They present a system which prioritizes the values and symbols of life which secures the lives of the non-marginalized and limits the control over destiny to elites. "Existence with" will of its nature demand some measure of institutionalization, but institutionalization must be forever reviewed, critiqued, revolutionized and changed lest it become an end in itself and lest it produce an "existence with" devoid of authentic equality.

Brokenness: A Personal Parenthesis

"Thanks for calling," she said to me, "I'm really worried about Tommy . . . I just can't understand it . . . He wasn't even out that night . . ." Tommy is in prison, he was taken there during the Liverpool riots of the summer of 1981. I have called on this little warm and welcoming house in the backstreets of Toxteth, just across the road from where I live. I am calling also because I am a prison chaplain. I go through the usual sympathetic mumblings. Then the mother continues: "You know the Magistrate said he was from a broken home; they've got to say that, haven't they?" I look around the home and feel nothing but peace. Then she says to me, "It's not his home that's broken, it's this area that's broken". I left and have since thought of the words of Marcel,

> "Don't you feel sometimes that we are living . . . if you can call it living . . . in a broken world? Yes, broken like a broken watch. The mainspring has stopped working. Just to look at it, nothing has changed. Everything is in place. But put the watch to your ear, and you don't hear any ticking. You know what I am talking about, the world, what we call the world, the world of human creatures . . . it seems to me that it must have had a heart at one time, but today you would say the heart had stopped beating."[1]

Actually let us say the heart is still beating in many breasts. But there is such vast puzzlement in the midst of the vast social, political and economic mess in which we are called to live. The heart is unable to beat with the infinite ticking which is its nature. That mother cried that day, or better, a few tears trickled down her face. You might call them "Stabat Mater" tears, tears belonging to a perceptive though silent vigil beside a broken world. She was perceptive enough to distinguish between the broken home and the broken world.

I remember how often the blame for rioting was left on the doorsteps of so-called broken homes; I remember well how easily certain politicians and political commentators shifted the cause of the troubles away from the institu-

---

[1]Marcel, G., *The Mystery of Being*, Vol. I, Reflection and Mystery, pp. 21-22, Harvill Press, Ltd. London, 1950.

tional collapse of society to the failure in personal responsibility of parents. This is not to say that parental authority is exempt from obligations and responsibilities. But like all the choices of living, such obligations and responsibilities can only be exercised within the context of the institutional world which they have inherited. And more often than not, especially within the marginalisation of inner cities, fullness of choice and responsible exercise of a role in life cannot be authentically exercised. The pain in such situations is to hear oneself, though firmly marginalized, being made to shoulder the burden of society's collapse. This is but another example of privatization versus institutionalization. It is a further example of that tendency in human beings, especially those of the elite minorities of this world, to run away from the task of institutional reform. We rush from such reform at our own peril.

Getting to Grips with the Institutional

To live the truly human life a reverential respect for history is surely important. The difficulty is making sure that such respect does not turn into enslavement. Authentic memory has a habit of slipping into a romantic nostalgia. Not only am I called to be critical of my present, there is also a like demand to be critical of my past. What I have inherited cannot be allowed to escape my efforts at criticism.

"The Western World in our age has been living under the dominion of two institutions: the industrial system of economy and a hardly less complicated system of politics which we call "Democracy" as a short title for responsible parliamentary representative government in a sovereign independent national state. These two institutions, the one economic and the other political, attained a general supremacy in the Western World at the close of the age preceding our own because they offered provisional solutions for the chief problems with which that age had been confronted. Their enthronement signified the completion of the age which had sought and found salvation in them; their survival bears witness to the creative power of our predecessors; and we who did not create them, have grown up under their shadow. In the industrial system and the parliamentary national state we still move and have our being; and the power of these two inherited institutions over our lives is reflected in the hold they possess over our imaginations."[2]

It is true each human being is born for infinity. It is equally true that I can make fundamental and radical choices which determine my life. I am also conscious of the reality of my own richness, in that I believe God has called me into a participation with him in a wonderful and inspiring task of creative power. All this is further enriched by my belief in the God who became part of my own human condition. Social, economic and political

[2]Trynbee, A., A *Study of History*, p. 30, Weathervane Books, N.Y., 1972.

theories, along with the structures and institutions which they spawn, cannot change such profound and breathtaking truths. Nevertheless they can bring about, existentially, a helplessness and hopelessness which bar and bolt the human spirit into a prison of living futility.

There is a terrifying tendency in humankind, at any stage of history, to grace fallible, temporary and mutable theories, and the structures born of them, with an infallible, eternal, and changeless form. This denies nature in the long run, its infinite yearning, and grace its divinizing power. Faith may well have victory in an imperfect world. But faith would be mocked if those who have power to make the world more perfect, selfishly agree to live with the imperfections to the detriment of the less powerful and the perpetuation of the totally powerless. It is for this reason that ideological and institutional criticism and change are part and parcel of the task of all those who would work for a more equal world. And, perhaps, at a more subtle level, it is equally important that those who so work ever remain reflective when it comes to their own alliances face to face with the institutions which we have inherited. If inherited institutions are challenged, one needs to be very careful that one does not give the benefit of the doubt to the institutions. Labelling and stigmatizing those who work for radical change seems to come easy to too many human lips.

One of the fundamental weaknesses in most analyses of the question of powerlessness, (I prefer to remain with this term instead of the term poverty), is the identification

of the word or concept "resource" with that of financial
income. Resource must be widened to take in other assets
belonging to an individual or a group. For example one's
social and educational relationships can be a vast resource
in life. Likewise one's environment can be a resource or a
non-resource. It is one thing to live in a totally rundown
neighborhood with all its inherited poverty and quite
another to belong to a neighborhood which is highly
developed. For one thing one's environment can produce
relationships beneficial to one's social advancement, the
other can plunge one into a permanent situation of
hopelessness. My access into or being part of the ruling
institutions of society, any society, will determine the
amount of power I have over my own destiny.
In the words of Townsend,

> "In all societies there is a crucial relationship between the
> production, distribution and redistribution of resources
> on the one hand and the creation or sponsorship of style of
> living on the other. One governs the resources which
> come to be in the control of individuals and families. The
> other governs the 'ordinary' conditions and expectations
> attaching to membership of society, the denial of or lack of
> which represents deprivation. The two are in constant
> interaction and explain at any given moment historically
> both the level and extent of poverty. The extent and
> severity of poverty is therefore a function, on the one
> hand, of the hierarchical and highly unequal distribution
> of resources, and, on the other, of the style or styles of

living which are constantly being defined and redefined and which a population feels compelled, or is compelled, to emulate."[3]

In a word, the institutions of society produce or demand a certain style of living. And those who can meet that demand perpetuate the power of the institutions. The interaction of institutions and style of living command between them access to the resources of life. Thus you may attempt to change the "willing", so to speak, of the powerless in society, but this is of no avail without a change in the institutions themselves. In 1970 President Nyrere, speaking to the Maryknoll Sisters, put the problem very clearly:

"The significance about the division between the rich and the poor is not simply that one man has more food than he can eat, more clothes than he can wear and more houses than he can live in, while others are hungry, unclad or homeless. The significant thing about the division of the poor and rich, and rich nations and poor nations, is not simply that one has resources to provide comfort for all its citizens and the other can provide basic services. The reality and the depth of the problem arises because the rich man has power over the lives of those who are not rich. And the rich nation has power over the policies of those who are poor. And even more important is that

[3]Townsend, P., *Poverty in the United Kingdom*, p. 917, Penguin Books, London, 1979.

social and economic systems, nationally and internationally, support these divisions, and constantly increases
them so that the rich get even richer and more powerful,
while the poor get relatively poorer and less able to control
their own futures."

It is not my task or purpose here to make an analysis of
the contemporary economic ills of society. But it is my
task, it is the one which I have taken to myself, to point
out that meeting the pain and suffering which marginalization creates in society demands I face the institutional
dimensions of our world and not be seduced into the
world of personal endeavor. Institutions have a habit of
breeding a view of life, "Well, that's the way things are
..." "You have to have society organised that way."

The U.S. and my country lived with this kind of
conviction for a number of years face to face with an
inherited institution. I refer to the institution of slavery.
Everybody did not have slaves. Yet slavery was considered as part and parcel of our institutional world. Yes, my
country participated in this view and actively promoted
it. Arguments on the "privatized" level were used to
protect it. Such remarks as, "The slave is happy ... it is
all that the slave can manage ... the master is good to the
slave," reduced the evil of slavery to a privatized level of
thinking. To be sure there was a great deal of self-seeking
in the abolition of slavery but at the end of the day it was
the institution itself which had to be abolished. But it was

an opinion that it was right and should be part of the social fabric of society. As Kenneth Stamp put it in his work, *The Peculiar Institution*, quoted by De Ste. Croix in his *The Class Struggle in the Ancient Greek World*,

"The (Old) South was not simply — or even chiefly a land of planters, slaves, and degraded poor whites. Together these three groups constituted less than half of the total southern population. Most of the remaining southerners (and the largest single group) were independent yeoman farmers of varying degrees of affluence. If there was such a thing as a "typical" antebellum Southerner, he belonged to the class of landowning small farmers who tilled their own fields, usually without any help except from their wives and children ... In 1860, there were in the South 385,000 owners of slaves distributed among 1,516,000 families. Nearly three-fourths of all free Southerners had no connection with slavery through either family ties or direct ownership. The "typical" Southerner was not only a small farmer but also a non-slaveholder. (Of the Slaveholders) 72% held less than ten slaves and almost 50% held less than five.

And yet,

Whatever the reason, most of the nonslaveholders seemed to feel that their interest required them to defend the peculiar institution (slavery as it existed in the Old South)."

But to take this argument even further.

One can be sympathetic with those who work for the amelioration of pain and suffering amongst the marginalized of society. I can assure you I am in that very business myself day by day where I live, work and reflect. To ameliorate or rehabilitate is all one seems able to do. And it is critically important that whilst we engage in cosmetic treatment we are expressing the opinion, and working towards, radical surgery socially, politically and economically. Let me give you an example from a particular aspect of my own life, one dimension of the suffering and pain of the marginalized Inner City.

The society which we have inherited and developed is one conditioned by the relationship between the employer and employee. It is not my purpose and this is not the place to question such a society "in se". But if it is that kind of society then unemployment is a marginalizing and alienating reality. In my own country it is a phenomenon leading to vast depression amongst people. One often wonders if one is creating the context for suicide. Face to face with this phenomenon, past political and present political administrations have launched government sponsored schemes for the young unemployed. This is good. I am on many of their management committees. But there is a grave danger that such schemes distract us from the need for vast structural reform on the whole economic front. Worse still such schemes could make the unemployment phenomenon invisible. The schemes are not in any way presenting a future in which the young person can invest. By hiding the evil we can put off the day for reform and radical change. Above all things one is being protected from asking fundamental questions about the values and the kind of society one wants. Some years ago, dealing with the question of the future of work, Fr. Chenu hinted at this when he wrote,

> "It is thus not merely a question of broadening the scope of classical morality, or drawing from 'eternal verities' marginal applications to suit the situation of the moment. We must revalue the new human terrain of work, which has become, in the machine age, a reality lacking anything in common with its previous character over thousands of years, its function and purposes are as much changed as its structure."[4]

Those words were written in the fifties. I would suggest that the change of the human terrain, on every front, has so changed now that the words of Chenu become even more crucial. One cannot keep attempting "marginal applications". The institutions of our society must be made to debate the fundamental issues of human living. They must be made to debate these even if the conclusion leads to the need for radical change. Left with vast questions it is too easy for such questions to be taken into the hands of the few, the hands of an elite minority, who make all decisions which touch upon the nature of life

[4]Chenu, M. D., *The Theology of Work*, p. 6, Gill and Son, Dublin, 1963.

and the power over human destiny. It is the paradox of our age that whilst technological advance has made communication easier, more and more decisions are finding their way into the control of fewer and fewer people. The signal for this is to be found in the response which is taking place in various sectors of society. Rioting cities cannot be brushed away with words like vandalism and "lefties". Human beings are simply saying that they have had enough. Above all, the marginalized are stating their God-given right to participate in creation of their world.

The Crisis of Participation

The pain and suffering of the powerless of this world, the pain and suffering of marginalization, are, I believe, to be located in the inability to participate in the creative process of this world. Buried in this statement is a warning for the insighted and well intentioned more powerful. This is absolutely crucial. But if this warning is taken seriously it means questioning the whole social educational process which we have come to accept. One is asking for institutional and structural change not only that the powerless of this world may get a better deal but also that *all of us* might discover authentic humanity.

There has been a rise in our times of what is sometimes called *Community Development*. It may be better to call it *Community Liberation*. The key to this movement rests in the preposition "with". It is not a question of the more benevolent in our society doing something about the problem of marginalization, even if that something is as profound as institutional reform, it is about doing something with the marginalized of society in order that all shall reach a true sense of being human. Thus it is not some far sighted people liberating the oppressed, it is about everybody together searching for liberation. If this preposition "with" is not grasped there is a subtle danger of being back with the privatized approach to the betterment of life. For "doing something for" can slip into mere charity, whilst "doing something with" has the stuff of justice in it. This "withness" is the only authentic beginning for real institutional change.

To refer to current questions: "Should Baby Doe live?" "Should the handicapped live?" "Should the teenager conquer the desire for suicide?" It may be as well to come to those answers with Baby Doe, with the handicapped and with the teenager. Suppose they all shock us by saying they do not wish to live. The answer cannot simply be, "But you must live!" The marginalized must be given the opportunity to question our grounds for that answer. It is to be expected that we will so answer . But it is only in dialogue with the marginalized that we are forced to look deeper into their problem of not wanting to live and therefore find ourselves forced to question our own predictable answer.

Let me attempt to put before you in order to illustrate this, the whole question of abortion. If I fight, in principle, to save the life of a child, I am faced with a further responsibility. It is the responsibility of making sure the world into which the child will be born will be a world in which there is to be fulfillment. Thus my fight for life must be a fight for total life. This means questioning my vision of life itself. One wearies of people who fight furiously against legalized abortion but abdicate all responsibility to fight as furiously for an environmental and social and spiritual world in which the child can grow to equal greatness. I remember well an argument about the causes of the Liverpool riots with a person who was very active in the anti-abortion lobby. She simply would not accept the fact that the causes of the riots were anything deeper than the irresponsibility of the parents of the area. This I must hasten to add is not to suggest that the fight for life is not a principle within itself. But it is to say that we cannot be selective when it comes to defining what the conditions are to be for the living of the authentic human life. Is the black child to have the same quality of life potential as the white child? Is the handi-capped child to know the same welcome into human community as the non-handicapped child?

Certain moral stands can be predictable in certain philosophies of life. The issue is that all human life be subjected to moral stands. If someone were to say "I will not bring a child to live and develop in this ghetto", it is not good enough simply to answer with the words, "But all human life is precious". I must go to battle with that person of the ghetto to change ghetto life radically. If I do not enter into such a dialogue and a subsequent partnership I am not joining in a search for the meaning of human life for *all of us.*

Lack of equal dialogue and future partnership I believe to be the roots of violence. If the marginalized of society do not see sincere and genuine potentiality to change in the life of the non-marginalized, then the development of life will end up in the marginalized seeking to become simply reproductions of the non-marginalized. One of the greatest problems of the opposition between the oppressed and the oppressor is that tendency of the oppressed to take over the role of the oppressor. In the situation of the oppressed and the oppressor both are dehumanized. It is crucial to understand this. In our marginalized and non-marginalized society of today both lose out in the field of human authenticity. Community, if it is true community, is about two essential realities, distinct yet inseparable. It is about searching for the meaning of human life and mutually shared power over life's destiny.

Community is not built or developed by bringing as many people as possible into the centre of life. Or to put this another way, Community is not about how I make the powerless of this world part of the reality from which I have benefited by reason of status, position or privilege. Community is about mutual enrichment of life by searching for authentic human values and sharing power over destiny.

This is a difficult agenda. Change cannot take place unless there is change in the lives of the non-marginalized.

I must take to myself, make my own, the pain, the suffering, the yearning of the marginalized. There is an extraordinary opinion expressed from time to time which seems to suggest that I can change the life of the handi-capped, the economically poor, the mentally suffering and all other categories of marginalized life without changing the life of the non-marginalized. Such a philosophy of life is rooted in an enduring charity perception of pain and suffering. It is rooted in that philosophy of action which sees activity as qualified by the preposition "for". When I allow my philosophy of action to be qualified with the preposition "with" I am moved into the world of justice.

But I cannot possibly act with, even exist with, the marginalized of this world without a drastic change in my style of living; such a change will inevitably demand a different view of the nature of the institutions and struc-tures of society. It is not a question of "seeing the problem differently", it is rather a question of "beginning to live differently". Pain and suffering and marginalization, and the pain and suffering which flows by nature from margi-nalization, are located not merely in the fact that a certain sector of people is not in the mainstream of human life, it is rather found in the view which states that such a sector of people have nothing to contribute to the mainstream of human life. As one of my prisoner friends who has suffered all his life from alcoholism put it to me: "I am a non-person inside and I am a non-person outside".

A Call to Mysticism

For twelve years I have lived and worked and attempted to reflect in the Inner City of Liverpool. I came there with a companion religious in 1971. It was my first major experience in adult life, of pain, suffering and marginalization on a social level. I say in adult life because I was a child in the same City in the depression of the 1930s. What I have written here has been written out of the experience of the past twelve years. As I come to the end of this chapter I must turn to something which I consider of supreme importance with regard to its contents. It is, for me, the logical outcome of my reflection up to the present.

Heidegger wrote in his *Being and Time*, "The question of existence never gets straightened out except through existing itself". If human existence is qualified through pain, suffering and marginalization, then that human existence, as a question, will never get straightened out except through an existence in pain, suffering and marginalization. There is a sense, and this I profoundly recognize, in which I can not cross that bridge of pain, suffering and marginalization. But I stand convinced that I must, in some way, cross it. I do not wish to suggest, for one moment, that such a conviction has neutralized either my life or my thought or my action. But I am convinced that we who are the painless, the non-suffering and the non-marginalized must find a way of crossing the bridge, if pain, suffering, and marginalization are to be prevented or alleviated. For, to refer back to a statement already made, I believe too many of us face the horror of our times by simply "seeing things differently". In other words we stand at the threshold of having to face conversion. I use that word with some deliberation, the word conversion.

In the last resort we need to find a union with the pain bearer, the sufferer and the marginalized. It is a union, like all authentic unions, to be established in knowledge, love and action. It is a new, late twentieth century mysticism. For mysticism is at heart about union subsequent to conversion. But though this will belong to the solitariness of the human heart it must have about it a sensitivity to the failure of institutionalization. For the Christian this means that the union with God must be established through the union with the pain, the suffering, the marginalization of too many people. Their deepest pain, suffering and marginalization is in the fact that too few seek such a union.

The values, the ideologies, which underpin our structures and institutions too often promote a self-securing of those who are already secured. Thus we the secured, too often unknown to us, become victims of our own ideologies and values. The human spirit thus becomes imprisoned behind the bars of its own chosen style of living. It unknowingly, this human spirit, sacrifices its yearning for freedom, authentic freedom. Selfish values worm their way into the human psyche in such a way that it seems unthinkable to choose against such values.

There is rumor still in the human soul, however,

making itself heard. It is the rumor which seems to say I have no right to all this whilst others bear pain, suffer and are marginalized. The whisperings in the soul are quietened by allowing the self to be moved from time to time to charitable acts towards the pain bearer, the sufferer and the marginalized.

In that union I will find the authentic liberation of the self for which I yearn. This is so because it is also in the spirit that the marginalized of our world also feel or sense their deepest pain. When the spirits of the marginalized and the non-marginalized touch in true seeking, an action becomes common; it is the action which searches for authentic human values and, for the Christian, therefore authentic Christian values. Thus liberation is mutual. Where we have been told that the Mystic of Christian tradition has been liberated by surrendering totally to God, so here I believe such liberation takes place when that surrender is through the powerless and marginalized of our world. Yet let's make no mistake about this. A price has to be paid. It is the price of a darkness of sense and spirit. It is a darkness which I take to myself now but which the marginalized are suffering already with an unspeakable intensity.

The past twelve years of my life have taught me one fundamental truth. I cannot seek God and the marginalized separately. I can only seek God with the marginalized by seeking as authentic a union as is possible with the marginalized. I believe this to be the mysticism of the contemporary Urban powerlessness.

Urban powerlessness is the specific experience from which I speak, can only speak. I felt this very deeply in the midst of the riots of two years ago in my own city area. I feel it each day now. If contemporary Christian men and women cry out that they shall not rest till they "rest in Thee", they shall not so rest until they have searched for that "Thee" in a union with the marginalized. I cannot expect that the marginalized will thank me for this search. They have nothing to thank me for. They have nothing to thank the institutions and structures of our world for. It is urgent that true community be established, a true community which will honor the uniqueness of the individual human person, and at the same time, out of a new consciousness, it will dictate radicalized institutions and structures, politically, socially and economically, which will set free the wonder of the human spirit. There is an urgency about this because our contemporary structures have led us all, marginalized and non-marginalized, to the brink of "nothingness". It is on this note of potential global destruction that I come to a close.

The Possibility of Nothingness

Although the nuclear crisis of our time is in itself an horrific and gigantic threat, a "negative par excellence", it has nevertheless within a positive power to move our thinking onto a more institutional level because of its very global nature. It has within it also the power to place before humanity an apocalyptical question, "At the end, what kind of values will you live for, which, in their turn, will make you believe you have something to die for?" If we wish to survive, what values are there in our world which determine that wish? Nuclear War is the ultimate conclusion of sick institutions, social, political and economic. The fact of the matter is the nothingness of the metaphysician has been translated into the daily anxiety of common man and woman.

Whatever contemporary man and woman can ignore, one fact they should find near impossible to ignore is the reality of death. One may validly say that this has always been the case. The funeral procession through our streets is part and parcel of human experience. The hearse does pass us most days of our lives. No matter how we attempt to disguise, architecturally dress up, our crematorium, we still must pass them on our walks, they are part of our social furniture. Death does stare us daily in the face and always has done so. But, I would suggest, there is a qualitative difference for contemporary man and woman. The actual furnace of the crematoria has been dwarfed by the potentiality of the mushroom cloud.

Humankind has proved that nothingness is a possibility. Worse still, even should all the nations of the world disarm tomorrow, have done with nuclear threat, the fact still remains that humanity has proved that it can "achieve nothingness". Even if we never step over it, we have been there. This places something in the global memory bank of humankind for all time. It can never evade it. The solitary individual in this situation is totally helpless. Any responsible individual, if this is what institutional, political, and economic life has brought us to, cannot avoid raising his or her consciousness to a constant awareness of the dangers of monolithic institutions and power seeking minority philosophies taking into their hands the destiny of human life. I believe we should positively reflect upon this on two levels.

Firstly, if we reject this potential nothingness, what do we intend to do with, how do we intend to approach, the "everything" which is around us. Above all, an essential part of that "everythingness" are the pain bearers, the sufferers and the marginalized of our world. Are they to be the first thought when we map out our plans for life and search for new institutions and structures, politically, economically and socially? Or are we to deal with them when we have devised our aims and strategies for a better world? Are the marginalized of this world to be an afterthought or are they to be an initial inspiring idea for a better world? Do we continue, as we do too often now, leave the marginalized to the sensitivity of certain individuals or do we build institutions inspired with sensitivity to them at the outset? How far are the powerful of this world willing to change their style of living in the name of the liberation of the powerless?

My second reflective point is intimately related to my first. And in offering it I trespass upon the grounds of the political theologian. In the Inner City it concerns me deeply. I use it to counteract the ever-present danger of privatisation face to face with the marginalised of our world. In the words of Metz writing in Volume V of *Sacramentum Mundi*:

> "Political Theology is a critical corrective of a certain tendency to confine theology to the realm of the private and the personal, as in its transcendental, existential and personalist forms . . . Political Theology is not primarily a new theological discipline among others, with a regional task of its own. And it is not simply some sort of 'applied theology' — applied to politics and human society. It cannot then be simply identified with what is called in theology 'political ethics' or with what was aimed at by the laudable movements of social theology or the 'Social Gospel'. Political Theology claims to be a basic element in the whole structure of critical theological thinking, motivated by a new notion of the relation between theory and practice, according to which all theology must be of itself 'practical', oriented to action. Only when this fundamental interest of political is ignored can it be mistaken for a theology dabbling in politics. . . ."

In a word, authentic Christian living, in its thought and action, must engage itself in the institutional and structural of our world. It is not an "abstract" or a phenomenon of comfort and consolation. It is there for social critique, social interpretation and social action. It is not there simply to contain the institutions of our world, it is there, when necessary, to change those institutions.

Above all things, remembering the Last Judgment scenario of Jesus, it is there to reach for the hungry, the homeless, the sick, the imprisoned, the thirsty and the naked. And it is there above all things to condemn those who would not take them as the first priority for life.

A BIOLOGIST'S VIEW OF PAIN, SUFFERING AND MARGINAL LIFE

by

Virginia Harrison

Marginal Life

Conversion has been described by the spiritual writer James Carroll as "to see through the eyes of another,"[1] I wish to share with you a view of "pain, suffering and marginal life" through my eyes, those of a fairly classical biologist and a person with a physical disability. The biological facts cannot give answers to human questions of value and meaning. They also cannot, by themselves, answer ethical questions. The view of life I can share with you may be a conversion, a new view that will allow you to put things in a new perspective. I may, with scientific facts, destroy some of the little havens where we've hidden from these questions, and we may help each other to discover what the questions really are; but biology can't give us the answers.

[1]Carroll, J.; A Terrible Beauty.

Before we begin to discuss marginal life, let me share with you how most biologists view life itself — simply life. How do we view it? With awe, with glee, with wonder and, somehow, with peace. We see life in a tremendous variety of organisms. Life can look like almost anything from a walking stick, to a peacock. It can exist almost anywhere: the South Pole, boiling springs, searing deserts. It changes more often than not; now it's a caterpillar, two weeks later, that same parcel of life is a soaring butterfly. Life has a rhythm, a propriety to it: those changes generally occur in a predictable order. At each stage, they can do those things proper to their time of life. Tough as life is, enduring as it is, life is also fragile, composed of delicately balanced processes, each very complex, each in harmony with the other.

Do biologists ever view life as marginal? In twenty years of studying biology I have never seen one reference to any life-form or any living system that was called or considered "marginal." Life itself has been called a metastable state. It is a very complex process, rather an "iffy" thing that requires constant input of energy to exist at all. When you realize the delicate balance of life, the luxury of labeling any of it "marginal" simply does not exist. It would seem a blasphemy to even think of doing so. We may say that an ecosystem is endangered, an individual is dying, an embryo is abnormal, a fossil is transitional, or a rare type is aberrant, but I don't think we'd ever call a life-form marginal. We are accustomed to lives that are very short, to animals whose immature and adult stages are very different from one another, to very small survival rates and to the aging process and death. We accept and respect all of these as valid expressions of life and proper to particular plants and animals at certain times in their life cycles. In the social scientific sense of the word, marginal denotes individuals who are not contributing members of the group. In biology we look for function but we don't use it as a prerequisite for life.

If a biologist did call something marginal, what would it be? Probably the viruses. For years there were great debates about the viruses. They definitely multiply. Your body gets invaded by a few viruses and several hours later, there are thousands, millions of them. They act alive. We also talk about "killing" viruses so they will no longer be infective. However, the consensus now is that viruses are not living organisms. They lack all internal machinery, or organelles, for maintaining life processes and carrying out their reproduction. They can only reproduce inside a living cell, using the cell's machinery and nutrients. That might fit one definition of marginal; they act alive, we kill them; but they can't do anything for themselves. I think we sometimes use these biological criteria to answer human questions and so act on half an answer. A virus, at its best, cannot love, cannot be loved, cannot worship.

Consider this story. I had a friend named Shirley. She had contracted polio in 1946. Shirley had partial use of one hand and arm, and could turn her head some. She spent her days on a stretcher, frog-breathing (that's a voluntary swallowing of air), and her nights in an iron lung. Like the virus, Shirley needed someone else to dress her, bathe her, push her stretcher, give her what she needed. Shirley was my partner in crime. She was the one who engineered the surprise party for a priest-friend and gave him "His and Hers" guest towels "in case the Pope ever changes his mind." Shirley was the one who could drink the double Bacardi before dinner because she didn't have to walk out. She was also the one who had an extensive correspondence with prison inmates, visited them often, and was active in pushing for prison reform. She had called, written to and met with quite a number of state officials on this matter by the time she died (of a cold) a few years ago. When I prayed about her death in church, people kept coming up and telling me "at least, she's out of her misery." Shirley wasn't miserable or marginal. She made a positive impact on more persons than some people ever meet.

I think the real issue concerning marginal life lies further up the evolutionary scale. We aren't wondering whether marginal people are alive or not; we're wondering whether they're human. Should a fetus have the protection of our laws? Should a criminal be killed like a dangerous animal? Is a person who cannot respond to us really one of us? Should we become emotionally involved with a disabled person? That's the question. How human are they?

To see this from the biologist's view, let's take it down a few zoological orders and look at the phylum Chordata (all animals who possess, at some time in their lives, a notochord, or cartilaginous rod rather like a backbone; i.e. sharks, fish frogs, snakes, birds and dogs). Because the notochord is the primitive form of an internal skeleton, these animals are well formed and capable of great mobility. For some adaptive reason or other, notochords are usually associated with cephalization. Chordates have distinct heads where their sensory organs are concentrated — that is, they have eyes and ears, noses and mouths just where you would expect them to be. Along with this goes a very well developed nervous system. These animals are smart and, usually, communication with one another is an important part of their lifestyle.

Are there marginal chordates? No, not according to the definition, but there is one chordate I've always thought was pretty marginal, the sea squirt. As an adult, this fellow is a vase less than an inch tall, who is glued to a rock somewhere, straining debris out of seawater. He has no head, eyes, or ears, and about as much intelligence as a sponge. We wondered what he was for many years. He certainly doesn't look or act like a chordate. The sea squirt was properly classified as a chordate when we discovered his life history. He starts out as a larva very different from the sedentary adult. The larva is a fish-like creature: very mobile, with a proper head-end, a notochord, and a fairly respectable nervous system.[2] Maybe the biologist's view of this animal will enlighten a few people: we would never dream of saying that the larva is only "a potential sea

[2]Kent, G.; *Comparative Anatomy of the Vertebrates* 1954.

squirt," or that the sessile adult "has ceased to be a chordate." I realize that, again, I'm giving you a biological answer to a human question, but this time, I think the concept that organisms normally go through quite drastic changes during their lifespan may be a helpful one.

Getting back to our "marginal" sea squirt; let's look at it from another point of view: that of a fellow chordate. *We are chordates.* The sea squirt can't do any of the things that we do, can't communicate with us, can't see or hear. Besides that, sea squirts are rather ugly, and usually covered with slime. We would rather not conceive of these creatures being in the same classification as ourselves. Even though the topic involves biological nearness to death, the concept of marginality is in fact a social issue. Biologically it wouldn't stand up. We would be much more comfortable if we could say that these people are not living fully human lives. We would like to say that they are marginal because they are really not like us. Therefore, we are absolved from human involvement in these situations.

To illustrate what the label of marginality feels like from the other side, let me share another story or two. I was born with spina bifida in 1946. In 1945 my parents had given birth to another baby girl, Ann, who had died within a few weeks from complications of spina bifida. Remember, I was born in 1946. In about 1967, I was a very successful college student, reading *Time* magazine, when I came across a report urging parents of a spina bifida child not to try to conceive again, because these children's lives just were not worth living. I wish you could experience what it is like to read in *Time* magazine that your life is not worth living.

Recently, I must have become a little infamous, for I was asked to be a witness in a court case. Evidently, when a handicapped baby is born and the parents don't want to treat it, one can persuade a judge to order that the child be treated by bringing in successful adults with the same problem. I'm glad people are doing that. I'm happy it works and very willing to participate. I'm honored that I qualify as successful. I am angrier than the dickens that you have to suggest that a child could become a college professor before you can get him medical care and a chance at life. Modern medical treatment is very good. The children now can often walk much better than I. Maybe this child can grow up to be a janitor or cook. Maybe someday a janitor or cook will be successful enough to testify in court on behalf of another baby.

I know what most concerns me about the terms "marginal people" or "marginal life." I get the feeling that we are describing some great, huge circle. At the center is some perfect stereotype — of ourselves. Included in the major central part of the circle are all the people and all the lives we feel are similar to our own. These people work for a living, they are married and have 1.7 children. They identify with a mainstream religion, but not too strongly. They have two arms, two legs, and are just taking up jogging. They are between the ages of 30 and 55 and haven't thought about death since grandma died

when they were 22. They don't have to justify their
existence to a court. Outside of this, what do we have?
Just the margins of our circle. The people who don't quite
fit. You're either in our circle or you're sliding off the edge
of the world — like the virus which has no organelles, or
the sea squirt which can't move. If you want to keep this
concept, I suggest you change the word. Pope John Paul,
in his recent visit to Costa Rica, spoke of "marginalized"
people. If these persons are on the fringes of life or society,
it is because someone put them there. Sometimes it is we
who put them there. By declaring them marginal, we
impact their lives in such a way that they can't approach
any closer to the norms of society. If we had truly human,
interpersonal relationships with them, we could not make
them marginal.

This concept of a single circle does a great disservice
not only to the people on the margins, but also to the ones
in the center who allow themselves to be stereotyped and
who believe the stereotype. I suggest that there is more to
human life than a single circle. We have been classifying
human lives as a biologist classifies animals or plants, with
rigid lines cutting a natural world that does not have such
clear-cut divisions and usually won't hold still long
enough for a neat dissection. Perhaps life is really made up
of thousands of interlocking, overlapping circles — and
we all live in several of them at the same time. If we think
of marginal people, or people living marginal lives in this
picture, then we have a very different image. They aren't
the ones who don't quite fit the mould, the ones sliding

off the edge. They are in the thick of things, integrating diverse aspects of life and of ourselves. They live in the overlap between circles.

This image of many overlapping, intertwined circles is my concept of what it means to be human. As members of this exalted species, made in the image of God, we are conscious of being unique individuals, gifted with higher mental faculties. We are also conscious of being part of the whole. To become fully human we need both of those experiences. Upon reflection, I think that I feel "most Ginny" when I am talking and thinking about exciting ideas; I feel really alive and in my natural element. This fits the biology book definition of human: having language and the ability to process abstract thought. I feel most human, however, most united with my species, and most in the image of God, when I am speechless. This happens when I, or a friend, have experienced something so good, so bad, so joyful or so sorrowful that it must be shared, but cannot be put into words. We embrace, we hold hands, we jump up and down and giggle. We gaze into one another's eyes. These are the two sides of the coin of humanness. We are each our own circle, but we must intertwine and overlap.

Father Thomas Swift, S.J., who is very active in workshops to help groups find and form community, says that "all people are interdependent. Handicapped people simply have fewer illusions about it." I think that many of the happenings that we are here to study simply place a person in that situation. The fetus, the disabled person, the person in great emotional or physical pain, the dying; all have no illusions about self sufficiency. They know they are dependent on others and they respond to those others as best they can. I could argue that they allow others to help them (we all need to do that) or that their existence teaches us of our interdependence and that is their worth (that their value lies in what we can get from their lives). I'm not saying that. I'm saying that interdependence *is* humanness. Because of their lack of illusions about autonomy, marginal people are, perhaps, the most human. If we do not respond to them it is we who are marginally human.

To illustrate the intertwining effect of interdependency, let me tell you about Bonnie. Years ago, my roommate and I needed a housekeeper. We had bought a big old house and could not physically manage it by ourselves. A priest friend suggested we hire a young woman who was trying to readjust after the drug scene of the early 70's. That's Bonnie. She's "feeble-minded," a genetic term for very mild retardation with a polygenetic (rather than single gene, such as PKU) basis. She became an unwed mother and lives on welfare. Bonnie is my friend — not acquaintance, not project, not object of pity — my friend. I suppose that she could tell her work didn't make life easier for me, but rather, her work made life possible for me. I think my disability evened the educational scales enough for true friendship. We've been to the Art Museum, the Botanical Garden and McDonald's together. I get an understanding acceptance of my low moments from Bonnie that I rarely get from my fellow faculty. When her second child was born dead, I wept with her. I don't think most professors have the gift of a Bonnie and I know that our friendship is fully human. I see that friendship as one of the richly colored areas where two circles overlap.

If we want to be whole, to allow our circle to be full, we must interact and intersect with many circles that are not part of our stereotyped modern life. We must interact with the experiences of many marginal people. Real life — biological life, human life — does encompass such things as pain, limitation, simplicity, love, loneliness and mortality which we are able to ignore in a hectic, affluent lifestyle. Some of these are evil. Pain, limitations, loneliness are evil because they trivialize human life. They make it less than it could be. They can severely limit our abilities to do, to think, to worship, to relate to others. For this reason, we need to alleviate them whenever possible. We have a tremendous responsibility to one another in this regard. No matter how firmly we may believe in the mystical value of suffering it is never fair to "offer up" someone else's suffering. We need to enter into these experiences and try to help.

We also need to respect these experiences and the people who undergo them. Animals also experience such things as pain, loneliness, and the nearness of death. To be fully human we must not only "experience" them as animals do but also deal with them and integrate them into our lives. We can't equate eradicating suffering people with reducing suffering. We need to respect and foster the process of dealing with pain, limitations and death as one of the most intense and deliberate acts of our lives. This is one of the most human things we do and one in which we are likely to find the divine, and therefore to live most fully.

I cannot emphasize enough that endurance and acceptance are very active, lively processes. In watching them in myself and others these past few years I have gained tremendous respect for that thing which we so easily call "free will" or "the human will." The strength to exercise this will seems to come from three things: a sense of the presence of God, the perception of human love, and a sense that what one does makes a difference. We need to help provide these things to the marginal people who are engaged in this intense encounter with the very stuff of life.

Much of this article has been marginal to my academic field of biology and may have seemed like a harangue. If it has, I apologize. As a biologist, I sometimes get the feeling that people want me to give them a scientific definition that will ease their consciences, and that angers me. Sometimes I can reassure them. I can tell you that a brain-dead person is really dead and you are not killing them when you pull the plug. I can tell you that removing a respirator from an unconscious person who really has no hope of recovery to normal consciousness and independent respiration is probably really "letting nature take its course." In other cases I probably cannot ease the ethical burden. As a biologist I cannot tell you that a normal fetus or a handicapped newborn is not human. I cannot tell you that a dying person or a severely disabled person is really dead already. I cannot say that a person who has murdered or who has taken his own life was not functioning as a biological human. I must proclaim that all these groups of people are indeed alive and are indeed human. I cannot say that they are "marginal." There may be situations in which we feel we need to end those lives for our own self-defense; be it physical, emotional or financial self-defense. In any case we need to face our reality and deal with it. We ought not to change the topic by questioning the classification of another person.

Pain, Anguish and Suffering

We have now, a number of significant points about so-called "marginal" life, at least from this biologist's viewpoint.

1) Marginality is a social concept, not a biological concept.
2) Marginality is a social condition imposed by some humans on other humans.
3) Each human life is valid and can only be judged from within the circle it creates.
4) Pain and limitation must be integrated into our experience to produce a full life.
5) Interdependence is a mark of human life.

Therefore, rather than marginality, in the rest of this chapter we will be dealing with Pope John Paul II's term "marginalization," the process by which people are put out of the mainstream of society and, sometimes, beyond life itself. If fetuses, persons in pain, persons who are lonely or limited in some aspect are indeed both alive and human, why do we marginalize them? Why do they allow themselves to be marginalized? The answer, I think, lies in pain, anguish and suffering.

After the first Stauros Congress, several years ago, I started thinking about the terms "pain" and "suffering." I tried to relate what I knew from my experiences of human life with what I knew from studies in animal behavior and the many new studies of natural analgesic systems. Pain was not too difficult to figure out. Suffering, defined as "to be for another," I was familiar with. I had seen love transform pain. I discovered, however, that I needed another category, that of *anguish*, to describe what I knew of life. Let me share my musings with you.

Pain

Pain is relatively easy to define. Animals feel pain — yes, even the little cockroaches I used to work on felt pain. It is a very unpleasant sensation. It can be physical, emotional or mental (though it is probably only physical in cockroaches). If a sensation causes you to weep, to cry out, to moan, and your first response is to try to get away from it — that's pain. Animals have pain and so do we, in about the same way.

We know now that there are two kinds of pain carried by two kinds of nerve fibers which make different connections in our brains. Each gives rise to different sensations and perceptions of pain. There are "fast pain" fibers which come mainly from the skin. They signal sharp pain. These connect almost directly with the cerebral cortex where we perceive exactly what part of our body hurts and how to get out of harm's way. This "fast pain" sensation has a very small emotional component. You can cut yourself, say "Oh my!" and rather dispassionately inspect the damage. If there is residual damage from the injury as in a cut or burn or if the pain is in deep tissues, the other pain system is activated. This system uses "slow pain" fibers which do not go directly to the cerebral cortex. We have a much harder time locating the pain and the emotional component of this slow pain system is quite large. Several hours after the cut, your finger is throbbing; you feel as if your entire being is concentrated in that finger and that the whole being hurts. The fibers from the slow pain system make diffuse connections through almost all of our midbrain and limbic system. This is the area that provides quality, emotion and response to sensations.[3]

We can easily distinguish these two perceptions. Fast pain is 1) sharp, 2) easily localized, 3) low in emotional

[3]Angevin, J., Cotman, C.; *Principles of Neuroanatomy* 1981.

content. Slow pain is 1) dull, 2) difficult to localize, 3) high in emotional content. It is this slow pain sensation which produces the phenomenon I call anguish.

Anguish

Anguish is the "angst" of psychoanalysts, philosophers and theologians. It is an added layer, overlying the pain, kind of an "epi-pain" phenomenon. When slow pain fibers from the spinal cord enter the brainstem, they excite the reticular system which keeps one alert and can make one very restless. Then they enter the midbrain and make connections with central gray matter and then the thalamus, and ultimately with the limbic system just below the neocortex. You don't have to understand all these fancy words, you can tell that these pain fibers affect nearly the entire brain. When stimulated, they can produce massive changes in neural processes.

All the brain structures we have met thus far in the slow pain system are classified as primitive; that is, they are found in older groups of animals, back, at least to reptiles. This indicates that anguish can occur in animals. When, in fact, one applies a painful stimulus to a rat, one sees behavior indicating that the rat is fearful, anxious, and interested only in escape. This response is mediated by the thalamus and limbic system.[4] This is a circular

[4]Kandel, E., Schwartz, V.; *Principles of Neural Science* 1981.

pathway in which the same impulse can evidently just keep going around and around. You have probably experienced this phenomenon in the emotion of anger which occurs in the same system. You feel like you are thinking in circles; you can't get your mind off your anger, but nothing seems to get resolved; you just get madder and madder. A very similar thing happens in the rat, or the human who feels anguish.

I think the feeling of anguish is much more intensely painful to a human, however, than it is to a rat. This circular system has two main entrances and exits, you see: the spinal cord and the cerebral cortex. Our cerebral cortex is vastly more powerful than the rat's. With our well developed consciousness and strong will we can send intense input into that circular system when we feel anguish. My first simple definition of anguish is that it is pain that you don't want. Think back to your last really bad headcold, menstrual cramps, migraine headache, or a longstanding interpersonal conflict in your family or community. Your whole being seems to ache. You say to yourself: "I wish this would go away." "Life is not supposed to be this way." "I don't think I can stand this." "There must be a way to stop this pain." "This can't be. There must be something I can do about this." "I can't take anymore of this." Each of these thoughts feeds back into the limbic system, perpetuating and intensifying our anguish. It gets worse and worse. This gives human anguish a unique depth and intensity.

This anguish phenomenon contains, as you can tell,

strong elements of anxiety and frustration which generally increases total body tension. This tension produces, on its own, more slow pain which feeds into the same circuit. All in all, anguish is "more painful," more difficult to bear, than the pain which engendered it. This is one of the reasons that relaxation techniques are so important in pain clinics. One can also decrease anguish reactions and even pain sensitivity in rats by teaching them that the pain stimulus is "inescapable."[5] I think this is one of the reasons that humans sometimes allow themselves to be marginalized. It stops the pain. This is a very primitive neural system and I think we relinquish some of our humanity when we use it, but it does alleviate some of the anguish. You don't have to keep looking for answers and restimulating that anguish circuit. It is analgesic to give up. I call this reaction "resignation."

Given that we have access to the anguish system not only by slow pain messages from the spinal cord, but also from our powerful cortex, humans are much more able to feel or intensify anguish for mental or emotional reasons. This allows us to feel anguish over the loss of capabilities, the loss of beauty, the loss of hope. If we retain our full humanity — that is, we don't resign ourselves — we behave much less like rats. According to Dr. Hans Selye, the easiest way to give a human peptic ulcers or any other symptom of *distress* is to put him in an unpleasant

[5]Graw, Hyson, Maier, Madden, Barchus; *Long-term Stress-induced Analgesia and Activation of the Opiate System; Science* 213:1409, 1981.

situation over which he has no control.[6] Technically, I suppose, ulcers are a sign of stress, but for our purpose I think they are also a reaction to anguish. To alleviate this added layer of anguish, people in pain need some power, some control over their situation.[7] This allows signals to escape from that circular anguish system and go either up to the cortex or down thru the spinal cord into action. It stops the reverberating, intensifying feeling. Dr. Selye calls the body's response to activity and achievement "eustress." This is a form of stress that keeps people alive rather than killing them. This escape from anguish is just what we take away from people when we marginalize them.

As an aside, this feeling of control is what makes bearable the pain of exercise, dieting or truly elective surgery. *We* decided to do it. *We* feel proud of our achievement and our self-control. And *we* can either decide when to stop it or feel confident that it is going to end. Unless we lose control, this doesn't lead to anguish. In contrast, even rather minor pain, if it is intractable or chronic, produces full-blown anguish.

Now, when a person is directly in pain — be it physical or emotional — often there is something one can do about it, or at least in regard to it. One can go to the

[6]Selye, H.; Stress; the Rotarian 1978. .

[7]Schulz, R. The Effects of Control and Predictability on the Psychological and Physical Well Being of Institutionalized Aged; Journal of Personality and Social Psychology 33:563 1976. Ramsay, L., Rayman, P.; Health and Social Costs of Unemployment: Research and Policy Considerations; American Psychologist 37:1116 1982.

doctor, receive therapy and make decisions. This activity in itself decreases anguish and probably sets one of our intrinsic analgesic systems into action. Dr. Brand spoke of this at the last conference.[8] We know now that there are several natural pain-killing systems which work under different conditions but there is one similarity in all of them: you need to have something going on besides the pain. Novelty, excitement, or productive work will all be effective. These neural circuits actually do decrease the pain and reduce anguish to a bearable level. I think they are often operative in the person with the pain. They probably are not working in the spouse, parent or child who can only stand and watch. A recent study of the spouses of cancer patients pointed this out. Their emotional pain is uninhibited by any of these analgesic systems. In addition, they may have a much higher level of anguish, characterized by a terrible feeling of powerlessness. In plain words, sometimes the onlooker's pain is the more difficult to bear.

This anguish may be most intense at the birth of a child with a severe problem. This is explained very well by John Fletcher in his book, *Coping with Genetic Disorders.* At the time of the birth, parents are all geared up, both by their biology and their culture, for a moment of joy.[9] Instead, they look at a whole lifetime of anguish in just a few minutes or hours. Their thinking and feeling brains

[8]Brand, P.; *Pain, To be Killed or Healed?*, Stauros Congress, 1981.
[9]Fletcher, John; *Coping with Genetic Disorders* 1982.

are completely overwhelmed by the anguish phenomenon. Medical decisions often need to be made when
they're having trouble thinking. Once some of the shock
has worn off, having information to learn and decisions to
make to help their child probably does relieve some of
their anguish, but even then, the medical personnel are
getting to *do* so much more than the parents that the
doctors and nurses get the greatest analgesic effect. In
addition, the parents have to function without knowing
that their child, if she lives, will develop with herself, not
their ideal baby, as her reference point. She won't feel the
same anguish of deprivation that they feel now.

A few years ago, a couple of us disabled adults were
called to talk with a woman who had given birth that day
to a handicapped child. It was amazing to see the difference between the grandmothers who were in deep
anguish, and the mother who, with tear-stained face, was
busy finding out how she could help her child and what
was available to him. I thought at first that the grandmas
had the luxury of falling apart and the mother didn't. I
realize now that, with a job to do and a way to help,
Mother was the fortunate one.

In summary, anguish is a layer of intense discomfort
overlying our pain. It may be triggered by deep or chronic
physical pain or by our own thoughts. It can be brought
on by the perception of pain in someone whom we love
and it is intensified by a feeling of powerlessness.[10] It is a

[10]Oberst, M. T.; Address to American Cancer Society Science Writers
Seminar, March, 1983.

self-propagating phenomenon which easily dominates our thoughts and feelings so that we can't do anything except feel this terrible anguish. It often seems overwhelming and, indeed, unbearable.

Suffering

Suffering has been defined as "to be for another." It is love. It is compassion, a "feeling with." It's the "He ain't heavy; he's my brother" phenomenon. I am beginning to think that some animals suffer, too. I think writing this paper has made me even more "Teilhardian" than I was. Perhaps, much of what makes us human is simply a more intense, conscious, and deliberate experience of many things that our friends, the animals, have done before us.

You will notice that in this section the impersonal pronouns disappear from my grammar. All the "ones" become "you" and "I." I cannot discuss suffering impersonally because it can't be impersonal.

Suffering involves pain too, often severe or long term, and anguish as well, but it is easier to bear than pure anguish is. You are either enduring pain to help, or to be with, someone you love. Sometimes the pain is a direct result of your effort to love. This is the case in parents, social activists and missionaries who often experience pain as they try to help their loved ones. At other times, you have the pain already but you decide to bear it in the faith that the Lord can somehow transform it into help for those who need it.

I think we can call either type of suffering "lived prayer" or "lived contemplation." In either case, you are putting your body or your life where your mouth is when you verbally pray for someone. You may be feeling anguish, but you give up that sense of power that is so important to relieve anguish. You give over your life to someone else. You accept pain; you say it is "OK" because it may help your friend. It still hurts and you acknowledge that, but you also acknowledge that it is bearable — and so it is.

We need to distinguish this from both the old idea of sacrificial penance and from the "offer it up for the Poor Souls" syndrome. I have personally found that if a particular person is causing me pain, I can only suffer it for that person. And, if I cannot suffer the hurt feelings in love, I cannot try to bear my sore shoulder in their behalf. I have also found that I cannot do it for myself. I can't try to suffer my own way into heaven, I need someone else to do that for me. I am also not usually holy enough, not so completely open to God, to be able to bear suffering for whomever the Lord chooses, or for some hypothetical "Poor Soul." It is much, much easier to suffer for someone you know, or whose situation you know, someone you love in a human kind of way.

I had a friend, Connie — a post-polio person, whose life was transformed by this. Connie could breathe on her own, but could only move the little finger on one hand. She lived in a nursing home and later in a hospital. We suggested that she pray and offer her life for others. Then, every time a foreign missionary came to town, every time someone was having trouble in the priesthood or religious life, we took them to see Connie. She could meet them, find out about their lives, care about them. From her small room, Connie's prayers and her suffering reached across the world. Her life and her pain were no longer meaningless; she had something to do with it.

As you can tell, I really believe that when we truly suffer, God transforms our pain and anguish into help for others *and also* makes it more bearable for us. As a biologist, I think I know part of how He does that. Remember anguish, and how our intense desire to stop the pain usually only makes the anguish worse? Well, when you suffer, you give up that desire for power over your own pain. You receive instead the feeling that you are a partner with the Lord, part of the healing power in the lives of those you love. That stops the vicious intensifying cycle of anguish and activates one of the analgesic systems to help inhibit those circular impulses. You still feel pain. You still feel anguish in the very core of your being, but it isn't spilling over, dominating your entire life. Suffering is peaceful. You know the pain may kill you, but it won't destroy you. In a very risky way, you are safe.

This anguish, I believe, leads us to marginalize others in an attempt to relieve our pain. We would rather not visit our critically ill friends because it hurts so much to see them. We would rather do things for a disabled person than watch them struggle with the task because it hurts to watch, and we often think of our own hurts first. As an example, a plush retirement home once asked a group of disabled persons not to come to Sunday dinner with their friends because it gave people bad dreams to see them.

Now that we have explored pain, anguish and suffering, I would like to put forward the following two-part hypothesis.

1) Anguish leads one to marginalize the person who triggers the anguish. 2) Suffering, on the other hand, leads one to include the person for whom one suffers.

The pain or disability we see in the lives of those around us can trigger either anguish or suffering. We look at the disabilities of others, without benefit of any adjustment or identification processes, and just know that "we couldn't take it." We see the pain of others, from our vantage point of powerlessness, and it is unbearable. So we decide that this really isn't living, or, if it is, it isn't worth doing. And it really is unbearable to us. It is terrible anguish.

Suffering, on the other hand, could never lead to marginalization. Suffering involves not only grief but also hope, for the Lord is helping. When we suffer for another person we are heavily investing our life in theirs. We won't say that their life is worthless because, in suffering, we gain the knowledge that our life isn't worthless. The circles of our lives have intertwined.

From these hypotheses about anguish and suffering, we can see ways to prevent marginalization of people by aiding those around them. We need to tell people in general that there may be mechanisms operative in another person which make his perception of the situation much different from their own. Most persons with disabilities, for instance, are very aware that there is more than one way to do any given task. They know, too, that whatever they can contribute to life is indeed valuable. Many terminal patients see dying as their last great task, to be done well — and they're not going to hurry it. If we can share things like this with people, they won't be quite so apt to marginalize people in order to stop the pain.

Those who are deeply involved need even more assistance. First, stop the anguish. See if there is something for the bystander to do to help so those anguish signals will stop going round and round in his head. Second, lead the friends into suffering. Help them to understand that, in more ways than one, their grief is that sacrificial love which the Lord can utilize to give aid to their loved one. Help them to see that continuing to love, despite the pain, is one of the most precious things they can give the loved one. They will still feel pain and still feel anguish, but they won't feel so helpless or so angry. They won't feel anguish about the anguish. It will be bearable. They won't have to marginalize anyone in order to stop the pain.

MARGINALIZING THE "RETARDED"*

by

Stanley Hauerwas

A Short Movie and a Question

The movie begins. A man and woman stand looking into a baby crib. The baby is never shown. The room is dark and the countenance of the couple is yet darker. They have obviously been through a trauma and are still in shock. The joy and excitement associated with the birth of a child has been crushed from their lives. Their high expectations have been transformed to absolute despair.

*Editor's Note: Except when the context demands its use, this article uses the terms "mentally impaired" or "mentally disabled" or "mentally handicapped" in referring to the condition commonly labeled "retarded", or the condition, "retardation." There is a strong, and legitimate movement underway to discontinue using the aforesaid terms because they not only inaccurately describe the medical condition of such persons, but are also offensive to the disabled persons and those most closely associated with them.

They turn toward us and the man speaks. "Don't let this happen to you. Our child was born retarded. He will never play the way other children play. He will not be able to go to school with other children. He will never have an independent existence and will require us to care for him throughout his and our life time. Our lives have been ruined. It is too late for us but not for you."
The mother speaks:

"Don't let what happened to us happen to you. Be tested early if you think you are pregnant. Maintain good prenatal care under the direction of a physician. Do not smoke, drink, or take any drugs except those absolutely necessary for your health. Please do not let this happen to you — prevent retardation."

A film very much like this was sponsored a few years ago by the American Association of Retarded Citizens. No doubt the film was made with the best of intentions and concern. Surely we ought to prevent a mental handicap. Certainly as many couples as can ought to be encouraged to maintain good prenatal care. Moreover the Association of Retarded Citizens is probably right to assume they will stand a better chance of getting research funds for such persons if they can convince the public, and thus the government, that their long term policy is to eliminate mental impairments as well as cancer. For if these can be eliminated then the amount of monies needed for constant care will be significantly reduced. Better a short term large outlay now than a continuing cost.

Nevertheless there seems to be something deeply

wrong or disturbing about this film and its message, "Prevent Retardation." Perhaps part of the difficulty involves the disanalogy between preventing mental impairment and preventing cancer, polio, or heart diseases, as these latter diseases exist independent of the subjects having the diseases. The disease can be eliminated without eliminating the subject of the disease. But the same is not true of the person mentally impaired. To eliminate the disability means to eliminate the subject.

Yet surely this point is not decisive. The film, after all, is not suggesting that we kill anyone who presently has such a disability. On the contrary those that produced the film have dedicated their lives to enhancing the lives of these citizens. They have led the war on unjust forms of discrimination against them. They surely do not seek to make their lot worse than it is already; rather they simply seek to prevent some from being unnecessarily born with this condition. What could be wrong with that?

Still I think something is wrong with a general policy that seeks to prevent it, but to say what is wrong with such a policy involves some of the profoundest questions of human existence including our relationship to God. In particular, assumptions about the nature and necessity of suffering, and our willingness to endure it in our own and others' lives, will need to be addressed. For the very humanity that causes us to cry out against suffering, that motivates us to seek to eliminate such a handicap, is also the source of our potentially greatest inhumanity. Why that is the case will take most of this article to explain.

Setting the Issues

Before addressing these large issues, however, I think it wise to discern more exactly some of the problems raised by the film as well as some of the problems of this film. It is obvious that the film is in serious conflict with the conviction of many that belong to and support the Association of Retarded Citizens. The film gives the impression that there is nothing more disastrous, nothing more destructive, than for a child to be born mentally impaired, but the sponsoring organization for the film maintains that these persons are not significantly different from the so-called 'normal.' Indeed, the Association for Retarded Citizens believes that with appropriate training most people with this disability can become contributing members of a society even as complex as our own. Thus the negative impression of "retardation" the film conveys is not one that those sponsoring the film believe or think warranted. And it could have the unintended effect of reinforcing the largely negative assumption about these persons present in our society.

Perhaps equally troubling is the indiscriminate use of the notion of "retardation" in the film. Not only does the film fail to denote the wide variety of the impairment —some much less serious than others, but even more it fails to make clear that our attribution of "retardation" may be due as much to our prejudices as it is to the assumed limits of the condition. It has become increasingly recognized that disease description and remedies are relative to a society's values and needs. Thus the term might not "exist" in a society which values cooperation more than competition and ambition.

However, the increasing realization that "retardation" is a social designation used too often to justify discrimination against those with an impairment should not blind us to the fact that such persons do have some quite specifiable problems peculiar to them. When the societal components of the diagnosis "retarded" are stressed, we can fail to recognize that these individuals are different in specifiable ways and that their difference requires special forms of care.

Yet it is extremely important how we put this if we are to avoid two different perils. The first, drawing upon assumption of societal prejudice embodied in all designations of "retardation," seeks to aid those so designated by preventing discriminatory practices in a manner similar to the civil rights campaigns for blacks and women. In this view, because they are said to have the same rights as anyone, all they require is to be treated "normally." Without denying that they have "rights" or that much good has been done under the banner "normalization," this way of putting the matter is misleading and risks making them subject to even greater societal cruelty.[1]

---

[1] For an excellent critique of the use of "rights" language in relation to retardation, see Barry Hoffmaster, "Caring for Retarded Persons: Ethical Ideals and Practical Choices," in *Responsibility for Devalued Persons: Ethical Interactions Between Society, the Family, and the Retarded*, edited by Stanley Hauerwas. (Springfield: Charles C. Thomas, 1982), pp. 28-41.

Would it not be unjust to treat them "equally"? Instead, mental impairments ought to be so precisely understood that those who are thus handicapped can be accommodated as they need.

That can be a reason for avoiding the word "retardation" altogether. As I have already noted, there are so many different ways of being mentally impaired, there are so many different kinds of disabilities and corresponding forms of care required, that to isolate a group as "retarded" may be the source of much of the injustice we perpetrate on those whom we identify as "not normal."

The second peril is that of oppressive care, a kind of care that is based on the assumption that these persons are so disabled they must be protected from the danger and risks of life. Such a strategy subjects them to a cruelty fueled by our sentimental concern to deal with their differences by treating them as something less than human agents. Too often such a strategy has resulted in isolating them from the rest of society in the interest of "protecting" them from societal indifference. As a result they are trained to be "retarded."

The challenge is to know how to characterize this condition and to know what difference it should make without our very characterizations of that difference being used as an excuse to treat them unjustly. In this respect, however, we see this is not just a problem in their case, but is a basic problem of any society since societies are only possible because we are all different, different in skills and different in needs.[2] Societies must find ways to characterize and institutionalize those differences so that we see our differences as enhancing rather than diminishing each of our lives. From such a perspective these persons are but a poignant test of a society's particular understanding of how our differences are relevant for the achievement of a common good.

The various issues I have raised can be illustrated by pointing to one final fallacy that the film underwrites. It gives the impression that mental impairment is primarily a genetic problem recognized at or soon after birth. But that is simply not the case. Half the people who bear the label, "retarded," do so as the result of some circumstance after their conception and/or birth. Many are mentally disabled due to environmental, nutritional, and/or accidental causes. To suggest, therefore, that we can eliminate "retardation" by better prenatal care, or more thorough genetic screening and counseling, is a mistake. Even if we were all required to have genetic checks before being allowed to marry, we would still have some among us that we currently label as "retarded."

We must ask what would a "prevent retardation" campaign mean for this group? If a society were even partially successful in "eliminating" it, how would it regard those who have become "retarded"? Since "retar-

---

[2]For example see my "Community and Diversity: The Tyranny of Normality," *National Apostolate for the Mentally Retarded*, 8, 1-2, (Spring-Summer, 1977), pp. 20-22.

dation" was eliminated on grounds of being an unacceptable way of being human, could those who remain look forward to a society able to recognize the validity of their existence or willing to provide the difference in care they require? Of course it might be suggested that with fewer there would be more resources for the care of those remaining. That is no doubt true, but the question is whether there would exist the moral will to direct those resources in their direction. At present we possess more than enough resources to care for all well. That we do not provide such care is not for lack of resources but lack of moral will and imagination. What will and imagination there is comes from those who have found themselves unexpectedly committed to care for a disabled person through birth or relation. Remove that, and I seriously doubt we will find any source in society that can provide the moral conviction necessary to sustain our alleged commitment to those with this disability.

To reckon whether this is mere speculation, consider this thought experiment. We live at a time when it is possible through genetic screening to predict who has the greatest likelihood of having a mentally impaired child, particularly if they marry someone of similar genetic characteristics. It has become a general policy for most of the population to have such screening and to choose their marriage partner accordingly. Moreover amniocentesis has become so routine that the early abortion of handicapped children has become the medical "therapy" of choice.

How would such a society regard and treat a couple who refused to be genetically screened, who refused amniocentesis, and who perhaps thus have a less than "normal" child? Would such a society be happy with the increased burden on its social and financial resources? Why should citizens support the birth and care of such a child when its existence could have easily been avoided? To care for such a child, to support such "irresponsible" parents, means only that the "truly" needy will unjustly be deprived of care in the interest of sustaining a child who will never contribute to societal good. That such an attitude seems not unreasonable to many people also suggests that in our current situation a campaign to "prevent retardation" might have negative implications for those who are mentally handicapped as well as those who may have the misfortune to be born with such a disability or acquire the same in the future.

Suffering and Those Who Are Mentally Disabled

But surely there is something wrong with my observation which seems to imply that since we can never ensure no one will be born or become mentally disabled, then we cannot try to prevent this at all. On such grounds it seems we cannot change our lives to insure that few will be born with the disability, so that those who are impaired now and in the future will not be cruelly treated and may even receive better care. Such is surely a vicious and unworthy position. We should surely rightly seek to avoid those forms of disability that are avoidable. To challenge that assumption would be equivalent to questioning our belief that the world is round or that love is a good thing. But like so many of our obvious beliefs, if we ask why they seem so obvious we often feel unable to supply an answer. Perhaps they seem obvious precisely because they do not require a reason for holding them.

I suspect that at least part of the reason it seems so obvious that we ought to prevent disability is the conviction that we ought to prevent suffering. No one should will that an animal should suffer gratuitously. No one should will that a child should endure an illness. No one should will that another person should suffer from hunger. No one should will that a child should be born mentally disabled. That suffering should be avoided is a belief as deep as any we have. That someone born disabled suffers is obvious. Therefore if we believe we ought to prevent suffering, it seems we ought to prevent mental disability.

Yet like many other "obvious" beliefs, the assumption that suffering should always be prevented, if analyzed, becomes increasingly less certain, or at least involves unanticipated complexity. Just because it implies eliminating subjects who happen to be mentally impaired should at least suggest to us that something is wrong with our straightforward assumption that suffering should always be avoided or, if possible, eliminated. This is similar to some justifications of suicide — namely, in the interest of avoiding or ending suffering a subject wills no longer to exist. Just because in suicide there is at least allegedly a decision by the victim, this does not alter the comparison with some programs to prevent mental handicaps: both assume that certain forms of suffering are so dehumanizing it is better not to exist than endure.

As I have indicated above, this assumption draws upon and is supported by some of our profoundest moral convictions. Yet I hope to show that as a general rule our assumption that suffering should always be prevented is a serious and misleading over-simplification. To show why this is the case a general analysis of suffering is required. We assume to know what suffering is because it is so common, but on analysis suffering turns out to be an extremely elusive object. Only after analysis has been done will we be in a position to ask if the mentally disabled suffer from their condition or whether the problem is the suffering we feel that they cause us.

The Kinds and Ways of Suffering

"To suffer" means to undergo, to be subject. But we undergo much we do not call suffering. Suffering names those aspects of our lives that we undergo and which have a particularly negative sense. We suffer when what we undergo blocks our positive desires and wants. Suffering also carries a sense of "surdness": it denotes those frustrations for which we can give no satisfying explanation and which we cannot make serve some wider end. Suffering thus names a sense of brute power that does violence to our best laid plans. It is not easily domesticated. There can be, therefore, no purely descriptive account of suffering since every description necessarily entails some judgment about the value of certain states or purposes.

For this reason we often associate, if not identify, suffering and pain. But pain and suffering are clearly not equivalent. If we are in pain we may well be suffering but not every pain is equivalent to suffering — thus some who feel great pain deny they are suffering.[3] But it is even more likely that I may claim to be suffering and yet be in no pain. Pain is neither a necessary nor sufficient condition for claims we or others are suffering.

I certainly do not mean to deny a close connection between pain and suffering; rather I only wish to challenge the assumption they are equivalent. Exactly how to characterize the nature of pain and suffering, as well as their relation, is no easy matter. Certainly it will not do to try to map pain and suffering in terms of objective and subjective elements of our experiences. Even though it may be the case that pain has physical correlatives that appear to make it more objective than suffering, pain nonetheless has a subjective side — what may be extremely painful for one may be less so for another. Moreover, suffering is by no means just the subjective side

[3]For a further analysis of the relation of pain and suffering see my "Reflections on Suffering, Death, and Medicine," *Ethics in Science and Medicine*, 6 (1979), pp. 229-237.

of pain, for we rightly believe we are able to attribute suffering to someone though they may not "feel" or think they are suffering. Such attributions are as tricky as they are dangerous.

In short, while pain may often be the occasion for suffering, it is by no means necessarily so. I may think of myself in pain, but not suffering. I may think of myself in great suffering, but not in great pain. That pain and suffering are often rightly associated surely is based on our presumption that each involves that which we undergo — what disrupts our projects or equilibrium — but that certainly does not entail the assumption that pain and suffering are equivalent.

But perhaps all this has put us off on the wrong foot. To look for a common meaning of suffering (and pain) may be a mistake. Simply because we have the word suffering does not mean it possesses a constant meaning or referent. In this respect it is interesting to note that most of the literature on suffering, at least in a theological context, seldom begins by offering an analysis of suffering. Instead the reality of suffering is presupposed in order to get on to the larger and allegedly more important issue of how innocent suffering can be understood or justified in a world claimed to be created by a good God. Without denying that much that is useful has been said about the issue, one cannot help but wonder if the cart has not been put before the horse since it is by no means clear we possess an adequate understanding of suffering, much less "innocent suffering."

No doubt the intensity of our own suffering or of our sympathy for others' suffering has reinforced our assumptions that we have a firm grip on its meaning. But it is by no means clear that the kind of suffering occasioned by starvation is the same as that of cancer, though each is equally terrifying in its relentless but slow resolution in death. Indeed, even the assumption that such experiences impose on us a common outcome is not as straightforward as it appears. It is interesting that we also use "suffer" in an active sense of bearing with, permitting, or enduring. While such expressions do not eclipse the passive sense associated with suffering, they at least connote that we do not associate suffering only with that for which we can do nothing.

Perhaps this is the clue we have been needing to understand better the nature of suffering. We must distinguish between those forms of suffering that happen to us and those that we bring on ourselves that are requisite for our purposes and goals. Some suffering which befalls us is integral to our goals, only we did not previously realize it. We tend to associate pain, however, with that which happens to us since it seems to involve that which always stands as a threat to our goals and projects rather than as some means to a further end. In like manner, we suffer from illness and accidents — thus our association of pain with sickness and physical trauma. Of course pain and illness are interrelated because most of the time when we are ill we hurt, but it is also true that conceptually pain and illness seem to stand on that side of suffering that is more a matter of fate than choice.

This distinction helps us to see the wider meaning of suffering. We not only suffer from diseases, accidents, tornadoes, earthquakes, droughts, floods — all those things over which it seems we have little control — but we also suffer from other people, from living here rather than there, from doing this kind of job — all matters we might avoid — because we see what we suffer as part of a larger scheme. This latter sense of "suffer," moreover, seems more subjective since what may appear as a problem for one may seem as nothing but an opportunity for another. Not only is what we suffer relative to our projects, but how we suffer is relative to what we have or wish to be.

In this sense suffering shares many of the characteristics and puzzles associated with luck. Like suffering, luck seems to involve aspects of life over which we have no control, yet we think some forms of luck are "deserved" or "undeserved." The latter judgment seems to imply that someone has led a life for which they "tempted fate" and thus got what they deserved.[4] We therefore seem to

[4]For a fascinating discussion of luck see Bernard Williams, "Moral Luck," *Proceedings of the Aristotelian Society*, supplementary vol. L (1976), pp. 115-135, and Thomas Nagel's, *Moral Questions* (Cambridge: Cambridge University Press, 1979), pp. 24-38. V. S. Naipaul has recently written, for example, "This element of luck isn't so mysterious to me now. As diarists and letter-writers repeatedly prove, any attempt at narrative can give value to an experience which might otherwise evaporate away." "Bogart, Hat and Popo," *Sunday Times Review* (May 8, 1983), p. 34. The question of the mentally handicapped thus depends on our having a truthful narrative that can form us as a people capable of being with and caring for those different, those who first appear as unlucky, from ourselves.

assume that certain kinds of suffering, like certain forms of luck, go with particular forms of life.

Without denying that the distinction between forms of suffering that happen to us and those that we instigate are requisite to our goals is important, we would be mistaken to press the distinction too hard. Once considered it is by no means clear if the distinction is as evident or as helpful as it first appears. For example, we often discuss how retrospectively what at the time looked like something that happened to us — something we suffered — but was in fact something we did, or at least chose not to avoid. Our increasing knowledge of the relation of illness to life-style is certainly enough to make us think twice before drawing a hard and fast distinction between what happens to us and what we do.

But the situation is even more complex. We often find that essential in our response to suffering is the ability to make what happens to me mine. Cancer patients often testify to some sense of relief when they find out they have cancer. The very ability to name what they have seems to give them a sense of control or possession that replaces the undifferentiated fear they had been feeling. Pain and suffering alienates us from ourselves. They make us what we do not know. The task is to find the means to make that which is happening to me mine — to interpret its presence, even if such an interpretation is negative, as something I can claim as integral to my identity. No doubt our power to transform events into decisions can be the source of great self-deceptions, but it is also the source of our moral identity.

Please note: I am not suggesting that every form of pain or suffering can be or should be seen as some good or challenge. Extreme suffering can as easily destroy as enhance. Nor am I suggesting that we should be the kind of people who can transform any suffering into benefit. We rightly feel that some forms of suffering can only be acknowledged, not transformed. Indeed, at this point I am not making any normative recommendations about how we should respond to suffering; rather I am suggesting the distinction between suffering that happens to us and suffering which we accept as part of our projects is not as clear as it may at first seem. More important is the question of what kind of people we ought to be, so certain forms of suffering are not denied but accepted as part and parcel of our existence as moral agents.

In spite of our inability to provide a single meaning to the notion of suffering or to distinguish clearly between different kinds of suffering, I think this analysis has not been without important implications. It may well be that those forms of suffering we believe we should try to prevent or eliminate are those that we think impossible to integrate into our projects socially or individually. It is exactly those forms of suffering which seem to intrude uncontrollably into our lives that appear to be the most ready candidates for prevention. Thus our sense that we should try to prevent suffering turns out to mean that we should try to prevent those kinds of suffering that cannot serve any human good.

Even this way of putting the matter may be misleading. Some may object that while it is certainly descriptively true that we find it hard to integrate certain kinds of suffering into our individual and social lives, that ought not be the case. The issue is not what we do, but rather who we ought to be to be able to accept all suffering as a necessary aspect of human existence. In viewing our life narrowly as a matter of purposes and accomplishments, we may miss our actual need for suffering, even apparently purposeless or counter-purposefull suffering. The issue is not whether inpaired children can serve a human good, but whether we should be the kind of people, that we should be the kind of parents and community, that can receive, even welcome, such people into our midst in a manner that allows them to flourish.

It may be objected that even though this way of putting the issue seems to embody the highest moral ideals, in fact, it is deeply immoral because the suggestion that all forms of suffering are capable of being given human meaning is destructive of the human project. Certain kinds of suffering — Auschwitz, floods, wars — are so horrible we are able to preserve our humanity only by denying them human significance. No "meaning" can be derived from the Holocaust except that we must do everything we can to see that it does not happen again. Perhaps individuals can respond to natural disasters in a positive manner, but humanly we are right to view such destructions as a scourge we will neither accept nor try to explain in some positive sense.

Our refusal to accept certain kinds of suffering, or to try to interpret them as serving some human purpose, is essential for our moral health. Otherwise we would far too easily accept the causes of suffering rather than trying to eliminate or avoid them. Our primary business is not to accept suffering, but to escape it both for our sake and our neighbors. Still in the very attempt to escape suffering, do we not lose something of our own humanity? We rightly try to avoid unnecessary suffering, but it also seems that we are never quite what we should be until we recognize the necessity and inevitability of suffering in our lives.

To be human is to suffer. That sounds wise. That sounds right — that is, true to the facts. But we should not be too quick to affirm it as a norm. Questions remain as to what kind of suffering should be accepted and how it should be integrated into our lives. Moreover prior to these questions is the even more challenging question of why suffering seems to be our fate. Even if I knew how to answer such questions I could not try to address them here. But perhaps we can do something better. I suspect that there can be no general answer to such questions that will not mislead as much as it informs. By directing our attention toward persons labeled "retarded", perhaps we can better understand what and how suffering is never to be "accepted" and yet why it is unavoidable in our lives. In preparation for that discussion, however, I need to try to suggest why it is that suffering seems so unavoidable.

On Why We Suffer

To ask why we suffer makes the questioner appear either terribly foolish or extremely arrogant. It seems foolish to ask since in fact we *do* suffer and no sufficient reason can be given to explain that fact. Indeed, if it were explained suffering would be denied some of its power. The question seems arrogant because it seeks to put us in the position of eating from the tree of good and evil. Only God knows the answer to such questions. Our task is to learn not to ask them, but rather to try to make the best of the fact that suffering goes along with being finite and, perhaps, sinful beings.

Without denying that the question of why we suffer can be foolish and pretentious, I think it is worth asking since it has such an obvious answer: we suffer because we are incomplete beings who depend on one another for our existence. Indeed the matter can be put more strongly since we depend upon others not only for our survival but also for our identity. Suffering is built into our condition because it is literally true that we exist only to the extent that we sustain, or "suffer," the existence of others — and the other includes not just others like us, but mountains, trees, animals, and so on.

This is exactly contrary to cherished assumptions. We believe that our identity derives from our independence, our self-possession. As Arthur McGill suggest, we think "a person is real so far as he can draw a line around certain items — his body, his thoughts, his house — and claim them as his own."[5] Thus death becomes our ultimate enemy — the intimation involved in every form of suffering — because it is the ultimate threat to our identity. Again, as McGill suggests, that is why what we suffer so often seems to take demonic proportions: our neediness seems to make us helpless to what we undergo. In this sense, our neediness represents a fundamental *flaw* in our identity, a basic inability to rest securely with those things which are one's own and which lie inside the line between oneself and the rest of reality. Need forces the self to become open to the not-self; it requires every person to come to terms with the threats of demonic power."[6]

The irony is, however, that our neediness is also the source of our greatest strength, for our need requires the cooperation and love of others from which derives our ability not only to live but to flourish. Our identity, far from deriving from our self-possession, or our self-control, comes from being de-possessed of those powers that promise only illusory power. Believing otherwise, fearful of our sense of need, by our attempt to deny our reliance on others, we become all the more subject to those powers. As we shall see, this has particularly significant implications for our relations with mentally disabled persons since we "naturally" disdain those who do not or cannot cover up their neediness. Prophets like these only

[5] Arthur McGill, *Suffering: A Test Case of Theological Method*, with an introduction by William May and Paul Ramsey, p. 89.

[6] McGill, p. 90.

remind us of the insecurity hidden in our false sense of self-possession.

It may be objected that such an account of suffering is falsely subtle since it is obvious why we suffer — bad things happen to us. We are injured in accidents, we lose everything in a flood, our community is destroyed by a tornado, we get cancer, an impaired child is born. These are not things that happen to us because of our needs, but rather they happen because they happen. Yet each does relate to concrete needs — the need for security and safety, the need for everydayness, the need for health, the need for new life.[7] If we try to deny any of these needs, as well as many others, we deny ourselves the necessary resources for well-lived lives and make ourselves all the more subject to demonic powers.

I have not tried in this brief and inadequate account of why we suffer to offer anything like a theodicy. Indeed I remain skeptical of all attempts to provide some general account or explanation of evil or suffering. For example it is by no means clear that evil and suffering raise the same

---

[7]For example one of the reasons the ARC film appeals to parents is the frustration parents feel when confronted by a child with a mental disability. Most parents suffer willingly for their children if they think such suffering will make their children "better." The problem with the disability is it seems to offer little hope of ever being decisively better. So we are tempted to eliminate such children because of our unwillingness to suffer for a child who will never get better. Of course parents of such disabled children soon learn, as finally all parents of normal children also have to learn, that they can rejoice in their children's "progress" even if such progress fails to correspond to their original ambitions for their children's "betterment." I am indebted to Rev. James Burtchaell for this point.

questions since certainly not every form of suffering is evil. Moreover, as I have suggested above, I do not think any explanation that removes the surdness of certain forms of suffering can be right. Much in our lives should not be made "good" or explained.

All I have tried to do is to state the obvious — we suffer because we are inherently creatures of need. This does not explain, much less justify, our suffering or the evil we endure. But it does help us understand why the general policy to prevent suffering is at least odd as a general policy. Our task is to prevent unnecessary suffering, but the hard question, as we have seen, is to know what constitutes unnecessary suffering. It is even more difficult, as with the mentally handicapped, when the question concerns another as it does in this case. It is just that question to which we now must turn.

Do Persons with Mental Handicaps Suffer from Their Handicap?

I suggested above that behind the claim we ought to prevent retardation lies the assumption that we ought to prevent suffering or, in particular, unnecessary suffering. By providing an analysis of suffering, I have tried at least to raise some critical questions about that assumption. But there is another issue that requires equal analysis: are we right to assume that the mentally impaired are suffering by their condition?

No doubt, like everyone, they suffer. Like us they have accidents. Like us they have colds, sores, and cancer. Like us they are subject to natural disasters. Like us they die. So there is no doubt that they suffer. But the question is whether they suffer from "retardation." We assume they suffer because of this, just as we or others suffer from being born blind or deaf. Yet it is by no means clear that such cases are similar or even whether those born blind or deaf suffer from blindness or deafness. Is it possible that they are in fact taught by us that they are decisively disabled, and thus learn to suffer? If that is the case then there is at least some difference between being blind and being mentally impaired since the very nature of this disability means there is a limit to our ability to make clear to them the nature of their disadvantage and the extent of their suffering. Of course that may also be true of being blind or deaf, but not in the same way.

Do these persons understand that they are mentally impaired? Certainly most are able to see that they are different than many of us, but there is no reason to think they would on their own come to understand their condition as "retardation" or that they are in some decisive way suffering. They may even perceive that there are some things that some people do easily which they can do only with great effort or not at all, but that in itself is not sufficient reason to attribute to them great suffering due to their particular disability. Of course it may be objected that if we are to care for them, if we are to help alleviate some of the results of their condition, we cannot help but try to make them understand their limits. We have to make them conscious of these limits if we are to help them be free from some of the effects of their condition. But again, this is certainly not as clear as it first appears, for it by no means follows that by learning to confront their limits in order to better their life, they necessarily understand that they are thereby suffering from something called "retardation," Down's Syndrome or the like.

Yet we persist in the notion that they are suffering and suffering so much from that condition that it would be better for them not to exist than to have to bear such disability. It is important I not be misunderstood. I am not suggesting that mental impairment is a minor problem or that nothing should be done to try to prevent, alleviate, or lessen the effects of it. What I have tried to do is suggest that the widespread assumption that they suffer from their handicap is by no means obvious.

Perhaps what we assume is not that they suffer from that particular disability, but rather, because of it, they will suffer from being in a world like ours. They will suffer from inadequate housing, inadequate medical care, inadequate schooling, lack of love and care. They will suffer from discrimination as well as cruel kidding and treatment from unfeeling peers. All this is certainly true, but it is not an argument for preventing retardation in the name of preventing suffering; rather it is an argument for changing the nature of the world in the interest of preventing such needless suffering we impose on them.

It may be observed that we have very little hope that the world will or can be changed in this respect, but even if that is the case it would be insufficient grounds for the general policy of eliminating such persons. On such grounds anyone suffering from treatment that results in their suffering would be in jeopardy. If justice comes to mean the elimination of the victim of injustice rather than the cause of injustice we stand the risk of creating admittedly a less troubled but deeply unjust world.

The need to subject this set of assumptions to rigorous analysis is particularly pressing in relation to the care of children born handicapped. A policy of non-treatment is often justified in the hope they will die and thus be spared a life of suffering. I by no means wish to argue that every child should receive the most energetic medical care to keep it alive, but if such care is withheld it cannot be simply to spare the child a life of suffering.[8] On such grounds few children with any moderately serious chronic health problem would be cared for at birth. We all, healthy and non-healthy, normal or abnormal, are destined for a life of suffering.

It may be objected that this is surely to miss the point behind the concern to spare certain children a life of suffering. The issue is the extent and intensity of the suffering. But again such a judgment is a projection of our assumptions about how we would feel if we were in their situation. But that is exactly what we are not. We do not

---

[8]For a more extended discussion of this issue see my *Truthfulness and Tragedy* (Notre Dame: University of Notre Dame Press, 1977), pp. 169-183.

know to what extent they may suffer from their disability. We do not know how much pain they will undergo, but we nontheless act to justify our lack of care in the name of our humane concern about their destiny. We do so knowing even that our greatest nobility as humans often derives from individuals' struggles to make positive use of their limitations.

I am not suggesting that the care we give to severely disabled children (or adults) will always result in happy results for themselves or those around them. But to refrain from such care to spare them future suffering can be a formula for profound self-deception. Too often the suffering we wish to spare them is the result of our unwillingness to change our lives so that those disabled might have a better life. Or even more troubling, we refrain from life-giving care simply because we do not like to have those who are different from us to care for.

Our Suffering of Persons with Mental Impairment

Why, therefore, do we persist in assumptions that those with the disability suffer from it? At least something of an answer comes from a most unlikely source: Adam Smith's *Theory of Moral Sentiments*. In that book Smith endeavors to provide an account for why, no matter how "selfish" a man may be supposed, there are evidently some principles in his nature which interest him in the fortune of others, and render their happiness necessary to him, though he derives nothing from it except the pleasure of seeing it.[9] Such a sentiment, Smith observes, is by no means confined to the virtuous since even the most "burdened ruffian" at times may derive sorrow from the sorrow of others.

That we do so, according to Smith, is something of a puzzle. Since we have no "immediate experience of what other men feel, we can form no idea of the manner in which they are affected, but by conceiving what we ourselves should feel in the like situation. Though our brother is upon the rack, as long as we ourselves are at our ease, our senses will never inform us what he suffers. They never did, and never can, carry us beyond our own person, and it is by the imagination only that we can form any conception of what are his sensations."[10]

It is through our imagination, therefore, that our fellow-feeling with the sorrow of others is generated. But our sympathy does not extend to every passion for there are some passions that disgust us — thus the furious behavior of an angry man may actually make us more sympathetic with his enemies. That this is so makes us especially anxious to be people capable of eliciting sympathy from others. Thus "sympathy enlivens joy and alleviates grief. It enlivens joy by presenting another source of satisfaction; and it alleviates grief by insinuating

---

[9]Adam Smith, *The Theory of Moral Sentiments*, edited by D. D. Raphael and A. L. Macfie (Oxford: Oxford University Press, 1976), 1, 1.

[10]Smith, 1, 2.

unto the heart almost the only agreeable sensation which it is at that time capable of receiving." [11] By knowing our sorrow is shared by another we seem to be less burdened with our distress. Moreover, we are pleased when we are able to sympathize with one that is suffering, but even we look forward more to enjoying another's good fortune.

Because we seek to sympathize as well as be the object of sympathy, Smith observes:

> Of all the calamities to which the condition of mortality exposes mankind, the loss of reason appears, to those who have the least spark of humanity, by far the most dreadful, and they behold that last stage of human "wretchedness" with deeper commiseration than any other. But the poor wretch, who is in it, laughs and sings perhaps, and is altogether insensible of his own misery. The anguish which humanity feels, therefore, at the sight of such an object, cannot be the reflection of any sentiment of the sufferer. The compassion of the spectator must arise altogether from the consideration of what he himself would feel if he was reduced to the same unhappy situation, and, what perhaps is impossible, was at the same time able to regard it with his present reason and judgment. [12]

We thus persist in our assumption that the mentally impaired suffer from that condition not because we are

[11]Smith, 1, 1.
[12]Smith, 1, 11.

unsympathetic with them but because we are not sure how to be sympathetic with them. We fear that the very imagination which is the source of our sympathy, on which our fellow-feeling is founded, is not shared by them. To lack such an important resource we suspect means they are fatally flawed for one thus lacks the ability to be the subject of sympathy. We seek to prevent retardation not because we are inhumane but because we fear the mentally impaired lack the means of sympathy. Exactly because we are unsure they have the capacity to suffer as we suffer, we seek to avoid their presence in order to avoid the limits of our own sympathy.

As Smith observes, we have no way to know what the mentally impaired persons suffer by reason of the impairment. All we know is how we imagine we would feel if we were in the same condition. We thus often think we would rather not exist at all than to exist as one in that situation. But as a result we miss exactly the point at issue. For the crucial point is that such persons do not feel or understand their condition as we do, or imagine we would, but rather as they do. We have no right or basis to attribute our assumed unhappiness or suffering to them.

Ironically, therefore, the policy of preventing suffering is one based on a failure of imagination. Unable to see like they do, to hear like they do, we attribute to them our suffering. We thus rob them of the opportunity to do what each of us must do — learn to bear and live with our individual sufferings.

Need, Loneliness, and Persons with Mental Impairments

In many respects, however, our inability to sympathize with such persons — to see their life as they see it, to suffer their suffering — is but an aspect of a more general problem. As Smith observes, we do not readily expose our sufferings because none of us are anxious to identify with the sufferings of others. We try to present a pleasant appearance in order to elicit fellow-feeling with others. We fear to be sufferers, to be in pain, to be unpleasant, because we fear so desperately the loss of fellow-feeling on the part of others. We resent those who suffer without apology; as we expect the sufferer at least to show shame in exchange for our sympathy.

As much as we fear suffering we fear more the loneliness that accompanies it. We try to deny our neediness as much, if not more so, to ourselves as to others. We seek to be strong. We seek to be self-possessed. We seek to deny that we depend on others for our existence. We will be self-reliant and we resent and avoid those who do not seek to be like us — the strong. We will be friends to one another only so long as we promise not to impose seriously our sufferings on the others. Of course, we willingly enter into some of our friends' suffering — indeed to do so only reinforces our sense of strength —but we expect such suffering to be bounded by a more determinative strength.

That we avoid the sufferer is not because we are deeply

unsympathetic or inhumane, but because of the very character of suffering. By its very nature suffering alienates us not only from one another but from ourselves especially suffering which we undergo, which is not easily integrated into our ongoing projects or hopes. To suffer is to have our identity threatened physically, psychologically, and morally. Thus our suffering even makes us unsure who we are.

It is not surprising, therefore, that we should have trouble with the suffering of others. None of us willingly seeks to enter into the loneliness of others. We fear such loneliness may result in loss of control of our own life.[13] We feel we must be very strong to be able to help the weak and needy. We may be right about that but we also may fail to be able to give the kind of help they really need. Too often we seek to do something rather than first simply learn how to be with, to be present to, the sufferer in his or her loneliness. We especially fear, if not dislike, those whose suffering is the kind for which we can do nothing.

Persons mentally impaired, therefore, are particularly troubling for us. Even if they do not suffer by their disability they are certainly people in need. Even worse they do not try to hide their needs. They are not self-sufficient, they are not self-possessed, they are in need. Even more they do not evidence the proper shame for

[13]For a further discussion of the significance of our sense of "control," see my *A Peaceable Kingdom: An Introduction to Christian Ethics* (Notre Dame: University of Notre Dame, Forthcoming).

being so. They simply assume that they are what they are and they need to provide no justification for being such. It is almost as if they have been given a natural grace to be free from the regret most of us feel for our neediness.

That such is the case, however, does not mean that they do not suffer from the general tendency to be self-sufficient. Like us they are more than capable of engaging in the self-deceptive project of being their own person. Nor is such an attempt entirely wrong for they, like us, rightly seek to develop skills that can help them help themselves as well as others. But yet we perceive them as essentially different than we, as beings whose condition has doomed them to a loneliness we fear worse than suffering itself.

That we are led to such an extreme derives partly from our frustration at not being able to cure them. We seek to help them overcome their disability but we know that even our best efforts will not result in a total cure. After all, what we finally seek is not simply to help them better negotiate their disability but to be like us: not disabled. Our inability to accomplish that frustrates and angers us, and sometimes they themselves become the object of our anger. We do not like to be reminded of the limits of our power and we do not like those who remind us.

We fervidly seek to help, to do for, to make their lot less subject to suffering. No doubt much good derives from such efforts. But our frenzied activity can also be a failure to recognize that our attempts to help, our attempt "to do for" must first be governed by our ability to do "with." Only as we learn to be with and do with, do we learn that their condition, our projection of their suffering, does need not create an unbridgeable gap between them and us. We learn that they are not incapable of fellow-feeling with us and just as important, that we are not incapable of fellow-feeling with them.

That such fellow-feeling is possible does not mean that they are "really just like us." They are not like us. They do not have the same joys we have nor do they suffer just as we suffer. But in our joys and in our sufferings they recognize something of their joy and their suffering, and they offer to share their neediness with us. Such an offer enables us in quite surprising ways to discover that we have needs to share with them. We are thus freed from the false and vicious circle of having to appear strong before others' weakness and we are then able to join with them in the common project of sharing our needs and satisfactions. As a result we discover we no longer fear them.

I am not suggesting that such sharing comes easily. Few of us are prepared to enter naturally into such a life. Indeed most of us, cherishing the illusion of our strength, must be drawn reluctantly to such a life. But miraculously many are so graced. Day in and day out, through life with their disabled child, brother, or friend they learn to see themselves through the eyes of the other who happens also to be disabled. Moreover by learning not to fear the others, they learn not to fear their own neediness.

Thus if we are to make a movie to help others avoid

unnecessary risks that can result in a mental impairment, let us not begin soon after the birth. To begin there is grossly unfair because it catches us before we are even sure what has happened to us. Let the film begin several years after the birth, after the parents have discovered, like all parents must, that they are capable of dealing with this. It is not the child they would have willed, but then all children turn out to be different than our expectations. This child, to be sure, raises particular challenges, but let the film show the confidence of the couple that comes from facing those challenges. Unless suggestions for avoiding disabled children are bounded by such confidence, we cannot help but make the life of such children that much more difficult. But even more destructive, such a campaign cannot help but make our own illustory fears of the other and our own needs that much more powerful.

An Inconclusive Theological Postscript

It may well be asked, however, what all this has got to do with our religious convictions as Christians? Of course there are some obvious connections that can be drawn. Christians are alleged to be concerned with the weak and the down-trodden. Those we are talking about fit that description. Our position seems consistent with such a religious sentiment.

Or it may be suggested that Christians are a people who have learned to accept that life is under God's direction. They attribute to God the bad as well as the good. Parents, in particular, think it presumptuous to try to determine the quality of their offspring. They accept their children, those with "good health" and those with "disabilities" as God's will. They do not presume arrogantly to ask why, or to what purpose, the latter children are born.

There is some truth to each of these positions, but they have to be stated much more carefully. The first can too easily result in sentimental acceptance and care of the disabled child in a way that fails to respect the integrity of their existence. It condemns him or her to being "weak" so that they might receive our "charity" rather than acknowledging them to be essential members of our community. The latter has been and is used wrongly to justify acceptance of avoidable suffering and injustice.

Yet these more obvious theological connections are not the most significant for helping us understand how we as Christians should respond to those who are disabled. Quite simply, the challenge of learning to know, be with, and care for them is nothing less than learning to know, be with, and love God. God's face is the face of the one mentally impaired, his body is the body of the one mentally impaired, his being is that of the one mentally impaired. For the God we Christians must learn to worship is not a god of self-sufficient power, a god whose self-possession is such that he needs no one; rather he is a God who needs a people, who needs a Son. Absoluteness of being or power is not a work of the God we have come to know through the cross of Christ.[14]

Arthur McGill has perceptively interpreted the classical trinitarian debate in this fashion. He suggests "the issue between Arius and Athanasius has nothing to do with whether God is one or two or three. It has to do with what quality makes God divine, what quality constitutes his perfection. From the perspective of self-contained absoluteness and transcendent supremacy, Arius can only look upon God's begetting a Son as grotesque blasphemy. God, he observed, must be very imperfect if he must generate a Son in order to become complete. But from the perspective of self-communicating love, Athanasius can look upon the dependent derived Son, not as a blot upon God's divinity, but as a mode of its perfection. Love and not transcendence, giving and not being superior, are equalities that mark God's divinity. Since giving entails receiving, there must be a receptive, dependent, needy pole within the being of God. It is pride — and not love — that fears dependence and that worships transcendence."[15]

That is why in the face of those who are mentally handicapped, we are offered an opportunity to see God for like God they offer us an opportunity of recognizing the character of our neediness. In truth, in this respect they are but an instance of the potential we each have for one another. That these men and women are singled out is

[14]McGill, p. 75.

[15]McGill, p. 78.

only an indication of how they can serve for us all as a prophetic sign of our true nature as creatures destined to need God and, thus, one another.[16]

Moreover it is through such a recognition that we learn how God would have his world governed. As we are told in the Epistle to Diognetus in answer to the question of why God sent his Son: "To rule as a tyrant, to inspire terror and astonishment? No, he did not. No, he sent him in gentleness and mildness. To be sure, as a king sending his royal son, he sent him as God. But he sent him as to men and women, as saving and persuading them, and not as exercising force. For force is no attribute of God." [17] But if force is no attribute of God's governance, suffering is. God, unlike us, is not separated from himself or us by his suffering; rather, his suffering makes it possible for him to share our life and for us to share his.

Our learning to share our life with God is no doubt difficult — it must be at least as onerous as learning that we can share life with those who are mentally handicapped. But that such a sharing of our sufferings as well as our joys, is necessary cannot be doubted. For a world where there is no unpatterned, unpurposeful suffering would be devoid of the means to grow out of our selfishness and into love. That is why, at least for those

---

[16]This sense of the prophetic character of those mentally impaired I learned from Dr. Bonita Raines' dissertation, *Care and Mentally Retarded People: Pastoral Dimensions Appropriate to Christian Ethical Convictions* (University of Notre Dame, 1982).

[17]Quoted in McGill, p. 82.

who worship such a God, we are obligated to live confident that we can live well with those whose difference from ourselves we have learned to characterize by the unfortunate label "retarded." For if we did not so learn to live we know we would be decisively retarded: retarded in our ability to turn ourselves to other's needs, regardless of the cost.[18]

[18]Much in this last paragraph I owe to Rev. James Burtchaell. I also need to thank Mr. Phil Foubert, Rev. Paul Wadell, C.P., and Dr. Bonita Raine for reading an earlier draft and making valuable suggestions for its improvement.

A PAINFUL ATTEMPT AT
AUTOBIOGRAPHY
MY "MARGINAL" LIFE

by

Harold Wilke

Pain and Its Uses

When I was two or three weeks old my mother carried me as she went about her weekly shopping in our little community. The town was small and stable: — People lived there and knew each other at least by sight reasonably well. As she walked toward the grocery store an acquaintance, a member of our church, stopped her and said, "Mrs. Wilke?" My mother said, "Yes" and the lady said, "Your baby?" and my mother rather quizzically said, "Yes?" At that point the woman said to my mother, "I heard the church bells this morning toll the death of an infant and I hoped it was your poor little crippled baby."

My mother's firm response was, "No, life is better."

The pain my mother experienced, not alone in that particular incident but in more than a few like that, was a pain that somehow was redeemed not by by-passing it, not by becoming a recluse, "staying home," but redeemed as we all can redeem pain, redeemed by an affirmation of life. "Life is better."

It was redeemed as well by her memory of what our physician had said at the time of my birth. He blurted out to her, "Mrs. Wilke, I have never seen anything like this in my life, I've never even heard of anything like this in my life." (He hadn't read the medical literature.) And then he added something that was an affirmation of his own feeling and of his assessment of her strength: he said, "I've never heard of anything like this, I've never seen anything like this, but somehow I am sure, knowing you, that it will be all right."

So pain counts, not in running away from it, but in its redemption — redeeming it by our affirmation of where we stand: where we stand in relationship to life itself.

Pain, then, is redeemable. Redemption may follow our pain. It may be that *your* pain, your problem, your difficulty, your anxiety, your suffering, may indeed be redeemed.

How could I ever understand the pain of my mother? How could I sense something of the psychological and personal suffering she went through? Her life had come unraveled. My father was numb, sandbagged by this thing over which he had no control and could do nothing about. My paternal grandmother, who lived with us, cried at the thought of me — for most of a year. It could even be that my mother had a deep sense of guilt in response to the hope expressed by the acquaintance, that the "poor little cripped baby" would have died. Maybe that was her secret hope as well, a hope that her Christian faith told her she should not have and about which she therefore felt doubly guilty. To the best of my knowledge any such doubts and any such half-formed hopes were never expressed, and resolutely she turned toward the next step, seeking out the future and its possibilities.

When, much later, some of the pain associated with societal response to the situation of disability came to me personally, I am certain that my responses were embedded by and sustained in the faith and positive response she had made at that point.

We need to look for a theological understanding of the problems of pain, to see these problems in relation to others in our society, and to seek the biblical and theological "reasons" for them. I title this section therefore, "The Uses of Pain." There is so much tragedy all around us, and within us, and we respond. What are, if any, the *uses* of pain? We need to put this personally and directly in our own life. What do we do with pain and suffering? What do we do with anxiety and disability? Can we look within ourselves and see the ways we have responded to the pain, the difficulty, the anxiety, the problem, everything else that society sees as negative? How have we responded? Let us, in our introspection, find some of the ways. I have related one such way, and I would like to add three or four more incidents related to the uses of pain, incidents that most of us can share in one way or another in our own life.

Trivializing Pain?

Does all this sound like just embarrassment? A teen at a prom? A college student rebuffed? All persons have embarrassment. There are layers and layers of pain, from being unable to remember a friend's name at a crucial moment to a sense that everything about one is unacceptable. Whatever layer we experience — it all dips into the same phobic pool that says *I* am not all right.

My experiences of pain could indeed seem to trivialize it when compared to the suffering of persons within catastrophic circumstances: Holocaust, war, oppression, Hiroshima.

But pain is always personal to the one who experiences it, and it is out of this perspective that I speak, out of what I know and experience. I may indeed project into the suffering of others and empathize, but in that I am still once removed.

So be it: I speak here of my pain, psychic pain, the pain of living with hurtful experiences. Unremitting bodily pain has its own cost, but I speak of what I feel.

To be sure it is the nature of my disability that physical pain is largely not a factor now, other than the occasional strained muscle from attempting to negotiate a too large log into the fireplace with one foot while stumbling on the other, or driving too long — one foot on the steering wheel — without a stretch and rest break.

The bumps inevitably suffered as an infant, learning in the usual kerplunk method peculiar to babies as they master balance and locomotion, and finally, walking were painful, I'm sure, when my top half, the center of gravity, got too far ahead of my base of support. (I could not catch myself with fat little hands and arms — as I later would watch each of my five sons do. I landed on my collar bone, my head, my nose, whichever touched down first. That broken profile of my Roman nose attests to a break in one such fall!)

So the pain of which I speak from my experience is the pain of facing the fact of my difference, and the even harder fact that many of those "normal" folk around could not either face or accept my difference. This fact is still a daily component of my life, but *most* days the frustration I face are not those of the judgment of my fellows, not even the frustration a physical world set up — and sometimes poorly at that — for persons with the usual component number of appendages, but instead that occasional rejection because of a difference seen as pejorative and negative.

Those pains, and the potential redemptions, go way back in my history, and relate to the following incident:

Some Uses of Pain

The incident occurred in my early attempts at dressing myself. Everything I need to do to take care of myself I do by myself, for myself. I travel alone and since my job last year took me abroad eight times, my wife cannot, of course, go with me. My wife, a smart woman, decides early that when I am to speak in North Dakota in January, her patients in psychotherapy really need her.

But if I am scheduled in Bermuda in January, she finds it possible to come along! So I am the lucky person too. Seriously, that total independence came about piece by piece as I coped with growing up as every child does who is given the precious opportunity to cope.

I was two or three years old, sitting on the floor in the bedroom of our home, trying to get a shirt on over my head and around my shoulders, and having an extraordinarily difficult time. I was grunting and sweating, and my mother just stood there and watched. Obviously (looking back on this from hearing about it a long time later), I realized that her arms must have been held rigidly at her side, every instinct in her wanted to reach out and do it for me. Yet she kept those arms tight at her side. Finally her neighbor, a woman friend, turned to her and said in exasperation: "Ida, why don't you help that child?!" My mother responded through gritted teeth, "I *am* helping him!"

Her pain in withholding help was actually a granting of help, in assurance that even though the pain and sweat level was high in the short run, it was being reduced in the long run. She expressed for me most graphically her own feeling that I must learn by myself. She helped me by not helping.

Still another redemption of pain is in seeking alternatives, in searching for new ways. After the immediate pain of knowing that a particular way is closed, seeking a new alternative, a new outlet, is redemption for that pain.

Such alternative-seeking happened to my father and

also to me. The one for my father came when I was excluded from school. The superintendent of the public school system said to my father: "Your son is not acceptable in the city school system." This was a shock for my father, who came out of that Rousseauan tradition in Europe through my great-grandfather. Thus my father, his grandson, was one who held the intellectual life of tremendous importance. For this youngster of his, then, to be denied schooling was searing. What he had to do therefore in finding a way out of his pain, out of an almost numbing shock, was to find alternatives. At that point he found the one-room country school house which I attended for numbers of years. The deep pain endured for him. In part the pain was there because the school board had simply held to the adamant stance of the first grade teacher, who stated: "No, we cannot accept this child. In all the fifty years I have been teaching here I have never had anyone like this who writes with his toes and I'm sure all the other scholars will be watching him all the time and therefore will pay no attention to their own lessons." (She certainly had learned little about the attention span of children during her fifty years of teaching!) That denial of education was felt even more deeply by my father partly because the response had a "circus act" atmosphere about it.

For me the alternative school was a great experience. I didn't know the complexities of what was happening, or what lay ahead for me. What did happen was the fact that I could attend that one-room country school house with all its special joys. For numbers of years I walked through two forests on the three-mile trek to school, across several streams, cutting through the pasture where the neighbor kept his bull (so that at least several times a year we had to run for it to escape the enraged animal). The very way I mention this shows how much I enjoyed the whole experience. I don't know how much I enjoyed my studies but I sure did enjoy going to and coming from school!

Some years later the rejection pain hit me. I applied to a college and was told, "We cannot have a crippled kid on the campus." The fact that within the week, I received an acceptance from Princeton may have alleviated the pain level for me somewhat. But the fact of rejection, the knowledge of the *reason* for the rejection, occasioned real pain. I know full well I overcame the pain, not by withdrawing, not by taking this denial "on the chin," but by bouncing back. I affirmed my own identity. I knew who I was and what my identity was. All of this I owe tremendously to parental and sibling response to me. It helped create a sense of identity to me, so that nobody, not even the president of some college or other could beat me down, because I knew who I was, and indeed, from my church relationship, *whose* I was.

Pain at this level has an element in it that draws out the resilience of the human spirit. It reaches out for us to affirm once again the identity which is ours.

But there are rejections which have nothing to do with whether we are accepted in a school but rather have to do with something at deep levels of intimacy, of what is proper, of what is esthetic. Such pain came to me when I attended the junior-senior prom. The high school gymnasium was filled with vari-coloured streamers —lovely indeed! It was a nice party; good singing and talk and all, and then we were sitting at card tables eating ice cream and cake. I eat ice cream and cake with my toes used for fingers. At that point my socks were cut at the end so that instead of looking like the mitten style I now use, all five little piggies stuck out. The front inch of the sock was cut off in order that I could both keep socks on against a mid-Western winter and at the same time be able to handle the pen and pencil and so on in school. That's the way I arrived that night. The picture included myself as one of the juniors, another junior off here to my right, a lordly senior across from me and our history teacher on one side. And I thought that Miss Wyatt looked at these bare toes with repugnance. I felt that she was in effect responding with some difficulty: "Bare toes don't belong on the table, in fact feet don't belong on the table." For more than a few months I had studied in her class with my foot on my desk, just as everyone else had their hands on their desks taking notes. But a party, a festive situation, was different, and she was unable to translate my action in the school classroom to the "dining room." I felt real pain that night. I thought that I was being looked down upon. I felt I was seen as boorish. At home after the prom that night I said, "Mom, we have got to change this. What can we do? How can we fix these socks so that on the one hand I can be comfortable in snow and on the other hand I can still have my toes free to write?" That night my mother and I invented the tabi sock. (We didn't know that the Japanese had invented it a thousand years ago, so we invented it that night for ourselves.) The mitten sock covered the toes, yet provided opportunity to grasp pen and paper. Again, it was a matter of finding alternatives; the pain was overcome in finding new ways. In some ways of course, the pain was twisted but it found a real expression in a new outreach so that the pain was in fact redeemed for me in finding this particular alternative. Alternatives do not reduce the level of pain, but set it in a meaningful context.

Still another of the uses of pain is the delayed response, a kind of acceptance of a temporary nature. It is the "holding pattern" response, in which the painful situation is accepted, one continues to live within it, and various means are sought to overcome the situation and to endure the pain.

The pain involved here is that of rejection within what is considered a very proper environment. It happened to me in my first year at college. I had been accepted (and spent my first two years at) a proud men's college in the mid-West, proud of its hundred years of association with a major denomination. A lifetime was filled in the first several days, meeting up with widely travelled and sophisticated young people my age, wearing clothes of such cut and quality that my suit, store-bought in a basically rural community, seemed really impossible. In the fraternity "rushing" days, a negative response, a "no" from one local group, did not actually get to me until the end of the week, and became almost a minor note in comparison with what was just then happening. Within the college dormitory the central figure was a professor who lived in "the dorm," and set the tone for the students there. Suave, handsome, totally "proper," he made me (and, I gather, a good many others) feel like country bumpkins by comparison. At that time I did not know he had his problems too; he seemed simply a paragon. And it was apparently his decision that I could not eat in the college dormitory dining room. I was assigned to a table in the hallway between the kitchen and the dining room, airy and light enough, but oh so obviously demeaning!

Should I leave? Should I hide? Should I fight back? I suffered in such anguish and agonizing depths that were the more so because I felt I could not share this with my parents. They would have felt so keenly for my pain — and I felt that somehow I could work it out better, uncomplicated by their outrage and hurt.

So I endured. I stayed with it. I remained in a "holding pattern."

Then the miracle happened: after some time students began to drift out to my own table in the hallway, and join me for chit-chat, later coming in for a whole meal, until finally there were numbers of us clustered regularly around that "beyond the pale" table.

At some point during this time the officials of the dining room and dormitory, recognizing a de facto defeat on their part, quietly gave in, and the system was abolished. In effect they said, "To hell with it!"

The useful response to pain, that of enduring, although probably not cognitively recognized by me, had made some change possible, both in me and perhaps even more in the administration.

The pain has endured, and my best memory is that I never shared this with my parents during their life-time.

Rejection for Ministry

Rejection for my chosen profession, the ministry, was still another painful denial. Strangely, I have had relatively little deep level pain connected with that rejection, because several of the rejections were contra-indicated by positive and accepting stances on the part of church leaders.

Thus, the very strong advice not to enter the ministry, given me by a local pastor of my denomination, came from a person whom I felt even at the tender age of fourteen or fifteen had no valid basis for his judgment —and indeed that he spoke out of his own ineptitude rather than his positive feelings for ministry. I witnessed this series of problems of his in relating to people, his difficulty in management of the congregation, and probably his lack of preaching skill. Thus, when he advised me negatively on studying for ministry, I felt he was saying, in effect, "Look, Harold, I can't even fulfill ministry adequately with two hands! How could you do it without hands at all?!" A piece of advice from an unconscious level was simply rejected by me, again at an unconscious level.

The negative advice from the president of the entire denomination — this was years ago! — was probably treated by me in the same way. The person did not know me; he probably was simply taking the word of that local minister whom I could not trust in his judgment about me; he was reacting to surface and immediate judgments.

To the contrary, a long relationship with a local pastor, culminating in a two-year study period for Confirmation, led to the strongest possible affirmation of my potential ministry, offered during the Confirmation service before a congregation of some five hundred worshipers.

Later, in Psychology 201 at the university, I could learn in personal tests of my negative suggestibility: we found a high correlation between a negative statement toward me and my rejection of it. How much of this rejection I could see as irrational is of course debatable; it may well have been varied blind spots in me, and an inability to face facts. But more deeply I felt at the time that I was expressing my own sense of identity, my perception of who I was and indeed whose I was — as indicated elsewhere — and the ego-strength posited in me at a very early age by parents and significant others.

The tests confirmed that I carried an aura of "I'm O.K., Jack," an identity strength which had become a strong base for me in meeting irrational negative responses. It was an armour-plate, admittedly with all the difficulties in wearing armour (inhibition of growth, loss of vulnerability, etc.) but it may have been my primary defense against "the slings and arrows of outrageous fortune."

Cathartic Humor

Laughter as a cathartic response to pain is still another of these uses.

It was a wry smile more than laughter that followed my experience with a Major General who insisted on opening the train door for me as we got aboard, in a voice that plainly put me well down in his perceptions of what a human being ought to be. The demeanor suggested that I obviously was crippled, needed help, and indeed out of his goodness and strength would provide it for me. In some dudgeon I started to open the door by myself, when I suddenly caught myself up short and said to myself, "Wilke, how often does one get a two star General opening doors for one?!" We walked through the whole length of the train, the General opening doors for me all the way, and I by this time smiling up my sleeve at the whole situation. In the same Pullman, he could not help but overhear the porter repeating three times a concern: "Can't I do anything at all to help you?", and my repeated asseverations that I was perfectly capable of taking care of myself and needed no help at all. The next morning the General came into the wash room just about the same time I had finished shaving. With the train lurching along at 80 miles an hour, and my standing on one foot as I shaved holding the razor in the other foot, I had not done a very smooth job but at least I had not cut myself. But the pay-off for me came when the very first thing, the General slashed his chin! At that point he felt impelled to apologize to me for feeling the night before that I had needed his pity and his help, that he should look down on me as a less than human person, as one who could get along only through his own largesse.

Laughter more raucous also takes place, perhaps somewhat more defensive in nature. But the humor response is basically seeking a perspective, nothing that the pain is part of an entire context, a whole pattern of response.

The Search for Understanding

Still another response to pain is to seek to understand why the pain exists, if it comes out of a human relationship. Such understanding delves into the motivations of people. It seeks out reasons for human response, especially when it is negative.

One of those responses in the use of pain has been described as the "pity and terror" syndrome, describing what happens when one person sees another with a severe disability.

The "pity and terror" syndrome comes out of a phrase relatively widely used in literature. Ahab and the white whale, The Elephant Man, and the Hunchback of Notre Dame symbolize the "pity and terror," an indication of how we have responded toward disability and particularly toward persons with disabilities. The response is not only toward the other person's disability but also that of the person with the disability toward his or her own situation.

It is self-perception as well as outward perception; it is a sense of response toward "disability" in general and that of the personal and specific.

"Pity and terror" is the phrase describing what happens when a "normal" individual sees a person with a disability and responds. To diagram this we draw an arrow from the beholder to the individual with the disability, with an arrow returning to the individual. There are two arrows, one pointing to the disabled person, returning immediately to the individual who is normal. Then follows the pity and terror response.

A footnote: When I use the word normal I always have quotes around it. The "normal" person is perceived by others to be normal or who himself perceives her or his own being to fit into that broad range of persons who basically are acceptable in our society. In point of fact, however, that broad range is not so broad: there are more atypical than typical bodies a medical doctor sees; but he still works in that range of what is called normal or typical. We are dealing here in broad terms and assumed perceptions.

The individual who perceives himself as abnormal or different, who sees himself as an individual whose difference is quite marked and draws from the "normal" person a response which is pejorative in nature feels the pity and terror response, seeing herself as causing it.

But such a picture is not true to the psychological facts of the response. Let us illustrate: Draw on a sheet of paper an arrow all the way across the page from left to right and then 1/16" under it another arrow right to left. Place at the left a round head for "normal" and at the right hand margin another round head — mis-shapen — for "abnormal."

That chart simplifies the process (and makes it simplistic): The normal person sees the non-normal individual, his line of vision comes back to him and he feels pity and terror in response to that other individual. That's the current, the accepted, the usual way in which such perceptions are stated.

I maintain that the picture is inaccurate. What actually happens is that one more turn of this arrow follows. When that arrow of vision goes over from the normal to the abnormal and then returns again to the normal person, the arrow then takes a sharp downward right-angle turn, a new line inside the normal head. The line continues down into the psyche, the unconscious of the individual who is "normal," then returns upward into the conscious, and then the pity and terror is evolved. Pity and terror, pity and fear, pity and anxiety are the person's own response to that within his psyche, within her unconscious. Returning to the conscious levels of the mind, the response is pity and anxiety.

The critical importance involves, among other things, that the individual with the disability does not create the pity and anxiety and fear in the other person. Rather, the person with the impairment only triggers something already there. The disability brings into consciousness for the non-disabled something in his or her own background, their own being, either from the recent past or far back in repressed memory, some experience that had not been adequately dealt with, that had not been fully assimilated in their life. The reponse is not to the person with the disability but to that un-assimilated or repressed painful experience.

This individual is like all of us human beings who have troubles, difficulties, anxieties and fears. They are rational fears, most of which we deal with in our normal life, and we work them through. The fear of the final examination, the fear of not getting the job, the fear of what the boss will say — all these are normal and mostly we deal with them. Where we have not worked through the difficulty, where we have been unable to deal with it and have repressed it, it needs only a trigger to come back once again to be a fear-creator for us. One little triggering incident will remind us of that un-dealt-with problem or anxiety or fear, long since, we thought, safely buried. That problem comes to the fore, to the conscious level, and once again creates all the old original fears that were so heavy that we had to repress it, to push it out of sight. It is the drawing forth again of an old difficulty. It's rattling around in the dry bones of an incident that happened a long time ago, or in the bloody bones of recent problems and difficulties which we thought we had repressed. These bones, these difficulties, have very special meanings for us, almost all of them negative and almost all of them causing considerable anxiety.

This happens to every one of us, to the person who is "abnormal" just as well as the "normal." It is the same for the person with the obvious disability as for the so-called "normal" individual. I will be personal. Harriet, a consultant to a group with which I work, and whom therefore I see once every two or three months, has fairly severe cerebral palsy. It affects her speech and her body. Her arms flail. She seems to have no control. So I come into the meeting and Harriet is there with her arms moving about somewhat uncontrollably and with her speech not easily understood. But I don't respond to Harriet's flailing arms in pity and terror, in fear and anxiety. I respond instead to what Harriet's flailing arms mean to me. What they symbolize to me is a fear of loss of control in my own life. I have, very personally, a real need to control. That need has been the subject of real dissension between at least several of my sons and myself over too long a time. My need to control is *my* hang-up, my difficulty, my problem, *not* theirs. That need is immediately brought to the surface when I see someone who seems obviously not to have control. Harriet's presence reminds me of what is for me a basic problem. I respond therefore in anxiety to a difficulty only apparently related to Harriet. Actually I am responding to myself.

The results of such understanding are manifold. It means a new kind of liberation takes place for the person with the disability and also for the so-called normal person. For me it's a new kind of liberation, a new kind of honesty in human relationships when I can see in Harriet's presence something of the reality of it; namely, as being representative of my situation rather than Harriet's. And this makes me see in honesty my personal relationship *vis-à-vis* myself, my inner being, and these two as related to the other person. We all have these relationships with many different people in our lives. It is important for me to know quite consciously that Harriet is simply symbolizing for me some of the difficulties of my life.

A whole new freeing for Harriet also takes place. The freeing for Harriet is her noting that I had actually withdrawn from her, did not like being in her presence, made snide comments, did any of the dozens of things that we do when we want to protect ourselves, when we feel ourselves in a fear or anxiety situation. It happened that all I did in this case was to push against myself. Many persons respond to such a situation by protecting themselves from the assumed aggression of the other, verbally or even physically.

Two illustrations: My British friend Catherine was thirteen at the time of this incident. Her mother had taken Thalidomide very early on in her pregnancy and Catherine was born with severely fore-shortened arms, and in a swimsuit her malformed arms are obvious. Catherine was at Brighton Beach and three other youngsters were there swimming. One of them came to Catherine and said, very aggressively, "What's the matter with you? What happened to your arms? That's funny; it looks awful." Catherine could have done two things there. She could have hit back verbally or she could have turned away. What she did was a combination. She explained, "Well, my mother took this pill so I was born with this difficulty." She paused, then said, "What's the matter with you, why do you squint the way you do?" Catherine protected herself in offering a reasoned response, but also she hit back, verbally, to protect her ego from the invasion of her privacy by the other individual.

All of us — all the time — respond to a person who is obviously different and perceived to be negatively different. We respond by protecting ourselves. The pity and terror syndrome evokes immediately correlative action on our part and that related action, physically or verbally, provides for us a defense against the assumed aggression of the other person. Actually of course the reaction is to the symbolic meaning of that other person's presence, not to the reality of that individual. The symbolic presence coming into our own psyche and rummaging around there among those dry bones or bloody bones draws forth for us that negative and fearful response we use to protect ourselves: by verbal sparring or by physical departure.

In my relationship with Harriet I have to the best of my knowledge not yet had to protect myself verbally or physically. She has never known the special meaning she has for me. I haven't had to walk away, nor make a snide comment. I have internalized the fear. But as soon as I understood the fear as being related to something within me then I have been able to deal with the outer fear and anxiety about Harriet. However, there are surely other places in my life where I have not responded by knowing the reality but have responded instead in terms of the fear.

Such opportunity for freeing, both on the part of the person with a disability and on the part of the person viewing the disabled individual, is highly significant. I have expressed this as a form of liberation in the first of those "Ten Commandments For Our Relationships With Persons With Handicaps" as I presented them to the United Nations at the opening of the International Year of Disabled Persons:

> "I am God, your Creator: I have brought you out of bondage. Liberation is a sign of the life I give you."

Analyzing the Negative Aspects of the System

Still another aspect of pain is the very system that religious structures themselves use to ostracize and reject. Churches have created a whole burden in religious faith, in proscription of persons for characteristics over which they have little or no control.

The Burden of Religious Faith

This burden is expressed in the widespread attitude of "fault" and "guilt" and "retribution for the sins of the past." Why try to overcome my handicap since it was inevitable and indeed ordained? This fault of a previous life or generation — this fault says I have no possible way of changing in the course of my present history what has been ordained because of previous history. There is nothing I can do about it. I am therefore without motivation to change — indeed I am almost required not to change but merely to accept.

Paying for *your own* sins expresses one's own sense of responsibility, of course, but also expresses feelings that since my guilt was there in the automobile accident which created the injury, I really ought to accept the consequences of my fault, and become the helpless person as a payment of the guilt which was mine. I have to pay for what I did wrong.

Another burden religion offers goes back to the Book of Leviticus, where in the 17th Chapter, God is quoted as saying that only the best can serve. No one may serve the bread of the Lord who has any physical defect whatever. The burden of that chapter has lasted for 2,000 years. It is in effect today. It is seen in the Orthodox churches, where Canon 77 and 78 clearly enjoin any handicapped person from becoming a priest. It is seen in the Roman Catholic church, where the doctrine of *"admiratio populi"* prevents ordination if any aspect of a man's physical being — blindness, being in a wheelchair, etc. — upsets the congregation so that it is unable to respond to him in his priestly capacity. Over the past 20 years, fortunately, Vatican intervention has made it possible for some 35 priests to become ordained even though they have a physical disability. In Protestantism, my own religious background, the pervasive refusal of congregations to accept persons with physical disabilities is a practice which is much worse than a canon or a doctrine.

We must remember that in this chapter of Leviticus the stress was not so much on pro-scription as on pre-scription: only the best should serve God! But still, this kind of teaching, expressed in all of the ancient Middle-East religions, is one of the great barriers religion sets up. If a person with a handicap cannot be a religious leader, how then is it possible for that person to be seen as a whole individual in the sight of the religious community.

There is also in religious understanding around the world a sense of fatalism: what is to be will be. What will come to pass will do so and there is nothing I can do to change this. Still strongly prevalent in North Africa, the Middle East and generally elsewhere in the world, this concept consigns the individual to a waste heap: acceptance of any negative aspects of his or her life. There is sporadic evidence that the mullahs in Egypt and elsewhere are attempting to change this, but the widespread influence is still present.

The resultant destruction or inhibition of the drive to overcome the injury, traumatic or (especially) congenital, is so obvious in religion that many doctors feel religion should be kept out of the rehabilitation center.

There is a personal reaction to the idea of *stigma* which tells the individual that he is wounded, that society perceives him as an outcast, and he must simply bear this burden and not attempt to do anything about it except to pay the tax. In the Middle Ages, certain persons handicapped in specific ways were simply required to pay a "cripple tax" on entering a medieval city. The cripple tax exists today, in society's difficulty in accepting handicapped individuals. The disabled person perceives this deeply, and therefore considers himself both unworthy and unable to do anything about changing the unworthiness. We have seen this happen. In Minneapolis, a small "religious" group is actually dedicated to saying to individuals who are blind, "If your faith were only strong enough, you could see." It happens all across the country. In response to such an arrogant and perverted statement, a Brooklyn friend of mine who is blind, retorts with biting sarcasm, "If *your* faith were strong enough, *you* could cure *me!*"

The Support of Religious Faith

Religion has the potential to supply acceptance, warmth and support in response to pain.

Ethereal music and dim lights notwithstanding, our faith concerns the hard-nosed reality of human existence; it is centered in the body. Faith begins in the incarnation, the crucifixion, and the resurrection. In those three words body is central.

The body, therefore, must also be central in worship

— eyes that can see, or if blind can be made in other ways to see; ears that can hear, or if deaf can be made through electronic or other means to hear. In order to make possible the fullest participation in worship, the church must provide eyes for those who cannot see, ears for those who cannot hear, and understanding for those whose intellectual function is limited.

The body is elemental; the act of touching is a natural expression. One priest, attempting to fulfill this concern, actually touches the hand of the recipient of the eucharist with his third finger at the same time that he places the wafer in it. And there are other ways to make touching a part of worship. The formality of tradition at present requires no such touching. Change, of course, must be effected cautiously; tradition cannot be dismissed lightly. Just as the sun can be looked at only through dark glasses, so looking at the mystery of worship requires the dark glasses of formal ritual. Yet our faith is body-centered. The Gnostic heresy, which held that Jesus was spirit only, was settled long ago.

The centrality of the incarnation will be symbolized in a special way by a priest who is disabled. Jesus experienced real suffering as a total human being. Why should not a handicapped priest represent the God who cares for one who is pierced, one who is broken, one who prevails in spite of hardship? A disabled priest incarnates the dying and rising of the paschal mystery. "What you are," said one early American philosopher, "speaks so loudly I cannot hear what you say."

In suffering, God and humankind truly come together. A handicapped presider, therefore, may do more than simply discomfit the congregation; he or she may serve as a symbol of God's own suffering over fallen humanity.

At the end of Vatican II, Paul VI gave a special blessing to representatives of several different groups who were not part of the mainline, including the poor, the lame, and the handicapped among others. Sitting in the Protestant observer's box, I watched in fascination the possibility that the church was beginning to envision a participatory ministry for such groups. Can there be an adequate ministry to a group of persons without also having a ministry with them? It is time to put Leviticus in perspective, and express in our worship the attitude expressed by Jesus that handicapped persons are to be fully involved within the worshipping community. Together we must do the deeds that God has sent us to do.

Liturgy planning committees can help to plan and implement greater participation of handicapped persons in worship. The scripture lessons are better prepared and proclaimed when they are seen against the background, the experiences, and the education of all the people in the church. Lay participation should include persons with varied handicapping conditions, both to be visible reminders that they form part of the congregation, and to share their particular insights concerning the preparation of the service and the conduct of worship. Here are a few suggestions:

When the worship committee or the parish council or

others carry the elements of the eucharist down the center aisle, some elements can be carried on the lap of the person in a wheelchair.

Some or all of the scripture lessons can be read by a mobility impaired or a cerebral palsied person.

Repetition in worship is of particular importance for many persons, perhaps particularly for persons who are mentally impaired. A liturgy that includes a procession involves both drama and repetition, and therefore carries its meaning strongly. Drama and repetition should be used more frequently.

We should make more of the equality of human persons, whether disabled or "able." All of us are sinners in the sight of God, and all of us are in need of God's assurance of salvation. If we, as members of a congregation, say of a crippled child or an otherwise handicapped person, "you poor thing!" we are in that confession also saying of ourselves that we are "poor things." In the eucharist and the sacrament of reconciliation, all of us recognize the shortcomings of our own lives, the blemishes of our own being. In all of our worship, the act of penance creates this common recognition, which may well be a basic tool for bringing all individuals into the mainstream of what it means to be church.

Within the liturgy numbers of litanies and responses exist that are dedicated to the church's ministries to persons with various kinds of handicaps. It is regrettable that many of these appear to be based on pity rather than equality. Many more are based on concepts of mission to, rather than mission with. Not having these persons as participants in the whole mission of the church to the world, however, handicaps the church itself.

Even when a church is architecturally accessible, so that a person who uses a wheelchair or crutches or has a cardiac condition can enter the church, why do we still submit to a style and order of worship which effectively prevents many persons from worshipping the very God who wants us to worship the divine presence?

Worship is aural and visual; it is intellectual and cognitive. For the blind, the deaf and the mentally disabled, worship as now practised often prevents them from taking that final step into the presence of the great mystery of God's love for us all.

Furthermore, there are places in Scripture clearly denying leadership in worship.

Surely the strongest proscription for the involvement of persons with handicaps in worship is found in Leviticus Chapter 21 verse 17 -23, where a long list is set forth of individuals who because of various kinds of physical handicaps may not serve the bread of the Lord. They may eat the bread, Leviticus points out, but they may not serve the bread: no leadership in worship is permitted.

The long arm of Leviticus says to us today that persons with handicaps may be brought into church — that architectural barriers may be broken down and they may enter to worship — but it effectively prevents those persons from actual participation from the chancel in mediating the mysteries of God. Whether it is the psychological discomfiture caused within the congregation by having a person with a disability lead in some aspects of the service of worship, or whether it is an architectural barrier that prevents their entering the chancel — that trinity of steps which is a problem for one in a wheelchair! — we seem to be saying today that Leviticus rather than Jesus was correct. Yet Jesus clearly stated the need of the religious community for total participation of persons with handicaps — and that surely means participation in worship both as the one receiving and the one giving, both as congregant and parishioner on the one hand, and priest or worship lay leader on the other hand.

The New Testament teachings of our Lord do indeed express not only the fact that he healed the sick, but that he included such persons within the community of the faithful. In Chapter 9 of the Gospel of St. John this is expressed clearly at several points: "*We* must do the work of the Lord." Jesus stated, "Neither sinned, but in this man's blindness there is still the possibility — yes, necessity — of glorifying God." The blind man even as blind remains one who proclaims the glory of the Lord. Jesus states that *all* of us must do the work of the Kingdom.

Growth, Nurture and Decision

To make a decision, within the context of pain, to respond to it, to understand it, to see beyond it, to rail against it . . . most of this implies and involves a decision. It is the decision of the paralytic (Luke, Chapter 2) that he would see Jesus, even to the decision of asking his four friends to carry him on his pallet to the house where Jesus lay. It went even beyond that: having arrived at the house, to see it full and a huge crowd pressed in at the front door, to have the decision — and the imagination — to take away part of the roof and enter in that way, certifies to a strong decision!

Jesus' response to the decision of the paralyzed man, this spinal cord injured person, is dramatic. He says, "rise and walk!" And the man, following up on what is surely a long series of decisions, does indeed rise and walk.

Learning how to make decisions comes early for most of us, growing from the decisions of parents as related to us, and decisions we make from small and seemingly unimportant events. These build upon and grow upon each other, to the psychological and spiritual strength of major decision-making later.

To help us see the continuing child and parent within our ego, we — all of us — talk occasionally with a parent who may of course be long gone. Some of my dialogues (with my deceased parents) are these:

"Mom, I did not learn until much later about what you both did for me in having my younger brother Harvey. Already present was my older brother Stanley, providing the immediate satisfaction and appreciation a child has for a playmate. But Harvey's birth gave me someone with whom I could fight, with at least some chance of winning, as one cannot with the older brother! True, I was supplanted — made second fiddle. I recognized that I was not the be-all and end-all, but Mom and Dad that's what you really did for me — you made me realize that even though I was handicapped you could still have another child. You did not have to centre everything on me. The feelings of guilt you would have unintentionally given me, whether recognized or not, would have been tremendous! You saved me from that, and I'm grateful.

"Mom, you did not know I would be born with a deformity. They had no tests in those days, no amniocentesis to tell you. But somehow I feel you would have had me anyhow and I would be here, a person, not a non-being. You said it later to that woman stranger who stopped you on the street, pulled down the blanket covering my torso and said triumphantly, 'Ah ha! I knew this was the deformed baby! It should have died.' You said firmly, 'No, life is better.' Mom, you affirmed that feeling again when a neighbor hearing the church bells tolling the death of a child said to you, 'I hoped it was tolling for your crippled baby,' and again you affirmed life."

My next word is with my father: "Dad, I was swimming just recently in the sea of Japan with a friend, and once again with gratitude remember your teaching me to swim as a little child. You really went to some trouble for your five-year old. Remember how you put together that four-foot board, tying an empty one-gallon syrup bucket at each end, telling me to place my chest on it and then push out into the water? In five minutes I had paddled across the pool several times and then discarded the support to launch in the deep, using the air in my lungs in place of the one-gallon containers. You said that I promptly sank, came up sputtering: tried again, sank again, but the third time I dog-paddled across the pool! Indeed, swimming is a joy for me. You assumed the ability, you took the trouble, and it worked.

"Dad, I understand your fear about my climbing up on the hay wagon that summer I returned home from college. It does seem ironic to me because for ten summers before that you had actually expected me to fulfill this needed task about the farm — bringing in the hay. It was fun to drive the horses along the field from one three-foot high pile of hay to another, and to watch you and Stanley and later Harvey pitch the hay onto the wagon with those long pitchforks. My job then summer after summer was to distribute the hay about the wagon and then to guide the team to the next window. It was not only fun — it was hard work and it was hot! We all sweated along with you. I knew I was participating in the family enterprise and it was a good feeling!

"But you tried to take away that feeling, unintentionally, I am sure, when I climbed up on the wagon as usual, that first summer home from college. You saw me in a new way, after a year's absence. You forgot all the help which you had expected me to provide in the past, and you saw only the problem and the danger of a handicapped child on the hay wagon. I certainly understand how your new-found fear about what would happen could over-ride your earlier recognition that I had to participate in family activity. Even close within the family you had to see me occasionally at least as a different person."

"You Trusted Me"

"Dad, you trusted me enough to teach me to shoot a gun. You may have been under considerable pressure from me and maybe even from Stanley and Harvey, because hunting was at least an occasional activity for us. Not so much hunting for game, my vivid memory is that of target shooting. I also have keen memories of being atop the cliff over the quarry lake in back of our home. I had the rifle, Stanely a shotgun, and Harvey a pistol. We lurked almost breathlessly waiting for those snapping-turtles that killed the fish to come to the surface for sunning. When that big body slowly came to the surface, we blazed away!

"Your very trust in me, carrying a rifle, provided for me another lesson, the sacredness of life, including animal life. You could indeed shoot a rabbit, but it had to go into the stew pot for supper. We never hunted simply for sport. Trapping was permitted only long enough for us to visualize the pain we inflicted on an animal.

"The care and caution one must use with guns is something you helped me understand even by the very way I learned to do it — sitting down, the gun butt against my shoulder, my left foot resting on my right knee and holding the gun barrel at the point of trigger, rather than way along the gun barrel — which meant I had to be even steadier than most persons."

Clarity and Understanding

All of us miss some part of our life, our job, our body, our person. What do we do when this happens? For some of us, it is coping, getting along with what we have. Using what is available to us, rather than sitting back and waiting for the right thing to come along, using a rusty blade if burnished steel is not available, finding reservoirs of strength within our bodies and our minds to take the place of some missing item, to develop more fully the strengths one has, to open another door — or even window — if a door has been closed to us. All of these are part of the coping process. Truly, "cope" is one of the great four-letter words in the English language, along with "hope," "love," "pray," "work," and "play." Many of you have discovered how to cope in the face of disability or problem or anxiety or other trouble. You have found the strengths deep inside you. You have recognized additional resources. You have developed new ways of fulfilling tasks when old ways have been closed.

For me personally, the "third eye" concept has been enormously helpful. The "third eye" is the eye of imagination, the higher stance we take to find new ways.

In dressing myself, without arms, I have not required

help since childhood. Using the "third eye" concept I experimented with and taught myself new ways of dressing myself.

The "third eye" suggests to me the alternative way: instead of putting on my coat and buttoning it, I button it and then put it on.

Here is how I get ready for each day: I put my trousers on, like everyone else, one leg at a time. But I secured the suspenders beforehand. Not quite fully secured, the trousers slip over my hips. I tie my tie before I put it on, slipping it around the collar of the half-opened shirt, duck into the shirt and tie together (or the shirt with a clerical collar attached), stand in front of the mirror on one leg and secure the shirt with the other, then pull the tie tight. Reaching into the closet for the coat, I lay it face up on the bed, button it with ten toes, flip it over, face down, duck into it as one ducks into a pullover sweater, shake it down over my shoulders and hips, ending the process looking normally dressed. Other arts of the dressing process are similarly fulfilled.

For all of us the possibility exists of finding the new way. With one door closed, we open another, or find a window or trap-door or ceiling exit. We open our minds imaginatively to receive the new and the fresh.

And we look deeply within ourselves to find and develop those resources which are present but so under-utilized. Our lungs have triple the capacity we ordinarily use. Our minds have limitless possibilities for thinking, our spirits un-told resources for fulfilling ourselves and our world!

The Under-Girding of My Religious Faith

Religious faith has provided for me the under-girding it does for any of us who call upon that strength, the strength to respond to the task. For me, two religiously-based understandings have been of enormous help:

The attribution or imputation of wholeness is the doctrine that says God sees us as whole persons, even with our problems or disabilities. The teaching is implicit in St. Paul, searching for a righteousness he could not secure for himself. Crying out "Oh wretched man that I am, who shall deliver me from this body of death?", he found that deliverance in God's free grace offered to him and to all humankind. That statement, called by Martin Luther the "Imputation of Righteousness" as a central doctrine of religion, has its correlation in the "Imputation of Wholeness." God sees you and me as whole, with nothing lacking, and no negative aspect present: made to be "without blemish in the sight of God" as Paul's letter to Ephesians points out.

Another teaching is that the disability is not as important as what we do about it. What forward steps do we undertake? What resolute forward-facing is ours? What goals, realistic, or some even mistakenly attempted, become ours? "Go and wash in the pool of Siloam" said Jesus to the blind man. We act! We do!

Perhaps most important, we do not immediately couple disability with sin. Always seeking for causes, we so often, even in the religious community, accept those old husbands' tales which assume sin as the cause of the disability. Jesus laid that old tale to rest two thousand years ago, in that same story of the man born blind. Responding to his disciples' question, Jesus said: "This man's sin, and that of his parents, have nothing to do with his disability."

Isaiah reminds us to "enlarge the place of our habitation, to lengthen the cords and strengthen the stakes." Our home, in earth and heaven, is to be constantly extended, stretched out. We are to go beyond our immediate armor plated protected place we now hide. We are to "build these more stately mansions, Oh my soul."

On a recent flight the stewardess noticed me sitting in the seat reading a book. Holding it with my foot, the watch on my ankle is plainy visible. She asked in amazement, "Wearing your watch on your ankle!?" I whispered back, "It's the latest style, right out of New York!" Smiling, she went on, only to return five minutes later, contrite: "I'm sorry, I did not notice you were handicapped — I only saw the watch on the ankle — and I trust I did not say anything to embarrass you." She had not, of course; all of us have learned out of our disabilities and problems to respond with equanimity to the strange responses of others.

But I did think about that wrist watch: how do you make an ankle watch out of a wrist watch? Very simply, by adding three or four links to the band. We expand the band. We stretch our horizons. We reach out to. the beyond. We enlarge the place of our mental and our spiritual habitation!

A REHABILITATION DOCTOR'S VIEW OF MARGINAL LIFE

by

Henry B. Betts

Marginal life has been described by some theologians as the pain and suffering of the powerless, the poverty-stricken, the handicapped, the institutionalized, the developmentally delayed and others who, for whatever reason, are unable to incorporate into society. In my remarks, I would like to look closely at that definition and talk about how well it fits the population I've spent my career treating: the physically disabled.

I've learned a tremendous amount from disabled persons. Our work in physical medicine and rehabilitation is not depressing. I see terrible tragedies that have occurred in life. But, I don't have to go to the Rehabilitation Institute to see terrible things. The handicapped do not have a monopoly on suffering. Moreover, I also see people struggling to find the very best in themselves.

These are major struggles. That process of finding whatever is the best — which is frequently better than

my patients every knew they had — is extremely stimu-
lating. Personally I'm very inspired by the patients I see. I
think they help me and the people around me to see life as
it is — to see people at their best, and to realize that there
is more good in people than most ever imagine, if they are
given the opportunity to search for it and express it.

When patients come to the Institute, they're usually
ready to be worked on physically. Often it's difficult to
say how long the rehabilitation process will take. Patients
are all different individuals, having different pasts and
different motivations. Yet, it would be very rare if some-
body had developed a severe disability and then was not
depressed for a while. This too is part of the process of
rehabilitation.

Very frequently they feel guilty. We see a lot of auto
accidents and other preventable situations where people
say, "I shouldn't have been driving with this person
whom I knew was drunk," or "I shouldn't have taken the
car out," etc.

As patients go through stages of depression, guilt and
anger, they tend to go on and work very hard. They
develop an awareness of their feelings and a sense of
identity. They develop an understanding of who they are:
their potentials and their limitations. This is how any-
body — not just the disabled — gets ahead in life. People
who live with illusions of what they look like, what
others' reactions are to them, and what their capabilities
are, probably aren't going to get very far.

Even armed with self-knowledge, patients are not

adequately prepared for re-entry into society. Self-knowledge isn't enough, patients also need to be taught to deal with the way society reacts to and categorizes them as disabled persons. Society views the disabled as living on the margin of society and unable to participate in the fullness of life.

Unfortunately, people have a way of looking in the mirrors held up by others. If they see the label "marginal," they are bound to feel marginal and act deprived. It is not unusual that people going into a down trend in their lives find that people avoid them. Patients in hospitals say that even doctors and nurses avoid dying people. They come to see them less. When individuals can't cope with someone who feels diminished, they tend to reject them, creating a self-fulfilling prophecy for the person feeling diminished. They feel diminished and expect to be rejected, they are rejected because they feel diminished. Feelings of diminishment tend to encourage rejection.

In dealing with patients, we try very hard to teach them about this mechanism. There is a tendency for some patients to feel when they go out into the world that it will be hostile and cruel, and that they will find rejection there. In many cases this is true. But those who are discharged from our care with this bias are the ones who are most often treated the worst. We constantly try to develop in our patients a sense of worth and identity. If we are successful in this, the patient leaves us with the skills necessary to elicit a positive response from the larger society.

However, no matter how emotionally complete a patient is when he or she leaves our care, there are still some aspects of society's prejudice which the disabled individual cannot control. During the International Year of Disabled Persons, the United Nations indicated that public attitudes about disabled people and disabilities in general are the major stumbling block handicapped people must overcome. I would take this a step farther and say that attitudes, labels, stereotypes and myths all tend to increase the burden experienced by the disabled.

The history of the handicapped is not a very encouraging or happy retrospective of human nature. Disabled people have been rejected from time immemorial — not only rejected, but sometimes discarded in harrowing degrees. The ancient Greeks threw disabled people from the mountains. The Japanese sent them into snowdrifts. Eskimos set them adrift on ice floes. Throughout history there have been violent discards of people who seemed not to be conforming and not able to be part of society, or who were considered, rightly or wrongly, not to be productive. Unfortunately, it is the larger society which sets the standard for determining who is "marginal."

However, there is no lack of irony involved in the way society perceives and treats the disabled. It is estimated that in the United States today there are over 35 million disabled people with at least half that number being severely handicapped. Ten years ago 15% of the working age population was limited in its ability to perform work because of a chronic health condition or physical impairment. Over 7500 people annually survive traumatic spinal cord injury. As many as half a million survive brain trauma, while over ¾ of a million live following stroke. Twenty million persons in this country are afflicted with arthritis and an estimated 17.5 million with back pain severe enough to require hospitalization. These figures don't include those who suffer from cancer and the 47 million Americans with chronic obstructive lung disease. Now, given these statistics, one might infer that the question is no longer one of what is marginal life, but instead how marginal is life?

The disabled are America's largest and fastest growing minority group. It's a minority that everybody who doesn't die suddenly or early is going to join. It will soon overtake others to become the majority. Is it ethical, moral or reasonable to label this population "marginal"? The difference between being on life's margin and not is hope. The individual who is impaired must find his or her own personal hope — wherever that lies. But he or she must also live in a hopeful society, one which is willing to contribute to the sustenance — not just maintenance —with the encouragement and the offering of love to those who are impaired. Hope is what makes marginal life a myth.

The hope for fullness of life which lies in the heart of the disabled has not gone unanswered. Disabled people are having an impact on medicine and on society. It's been proven to be economically feasible and sensible to rehabilitate people rather than support them in a custodial manner. Lay people, economists and sociologists realize that. I don't think that even forty years ago there were many reasons to assume that rehabilitation would be considered economically sensible. Whatever the definition of "marginal life" is today, it will be different tomorrow.

But what we are learning from the disabled goes far beyond the economics. At the moment the most common criticism of medicine is that physicians, and for that matter all staff persons who come in contact with patients, have turned to technology rather than humanism. They are avoiding *touching*, literally and figuratively. Patients tell us, "My doctor never talks to me; never listens to me; puts me in all these machines; and doesn't tell me what they're going to do. They don't tell me the results of what they do. They leave me in long dark corridors. They don't explain things and mostly they don't seem to care."

In rehabilitation you can't deal with the handicapped and deal only with technology. One wouldn't go into the business unless he or she were willing to deal with the whole person and everything that touches that person —because what you do medically and technologically is very minimal, frankly. Instead the physician must learn to deal with people and to understand them. He or she must be a master at listening and understanding. In a great many ways my patients are teaching young doctors about this. We now have a first year course in which we can take about 60 students at a time. Last term 250 students applied for that course so they could come and work with our patients and learn these skills.

Finally, we can do stunning things in our hospitals. It is easy for us to delude ourselves into believing that because people do well in our institutions we've performed miracles. We forget that in the end it's up to the patients. They're the people who must know about their capabilities and about what they and we can and cannot do. They've got to know about themselves in order to go on in life. Self-knowledge and hope are the two weapons which keep disabled people from being on life's margin. Unless we, as physicians, can encourage, develop, and instill hope and self-knowledge, then anything else we do will be meaningless.